Praise for *Simplify Everything*

D0912794

"Our research on business process dovetails perfectly with what Steve explains. We need to understand what makes money and what does not, then focus on getting the right things done. It is critical to the successful and sustainable firm of tomorrow.

—F. Barry Lawrence, PhD, Leonard and Valerie Bruce chair; director, Industrial Distribution Program; director, Thomas & Joan Read Center for Distribution Research and Education; director, Supply Chain Systems Laboratory, Texas A&M University

"At Purdue, we teach our students about the real world—not just theory. Getting a team to "done" is a major part of getting yourself to success. I stress to students and corporate clients that looking busy is not enough. Successful people accomplish tasks and reach goals with everything they do. Steve's book will help you get on the right path."

—Kathryne A. Newton, PhD, professor, Industrial Distribution Department of Technology, Leadership, and Innovation, Purdue University

simplify
everything

GET YOUR TEAM
FROM DO-DO
TO DONE-DONE
WITH ONE
SUREFIRE PROCESS

STEVE EPNER

LIVE OAK
BOOK COMPANY

Published by Live Oak Book Company
Austin, TX
www.liveoakbookcompany.com

Distributed by Live Oak Book Company

For ordering information or special discounts for bulk purchases, please contact Live Oak Book Company at PO Box 91869, Austin, TX 78709, 512.891.6100.

Design and composition by Greenleaf Book Group LLC
Cover design by Greenleaf Book Group LLC

Publisher's Cataloging-In-Publication Data
(Prepared by The Donohue Group, Inc.)

Epner, Steve.
  Simplify everything : get your team from do-do to done-done with one surefire process / Steve Epner.—1st ed.
    p. ; cm.
  Issued also as an ebook.
  ISBN: 978-1-936909-50-6
  1. Goal setting in personnel management. 2. Labor productivity. 3. Creative ability in business. I. Title.
HF5549.5.G6 E66 2012
658.314   2012937505

eBook ISBN: 978-1-936909-51-3

First Edition

This book is dedicated to the friends and clients I have met over the years. My favorites have always encouraged me to keep moving forward on my life's journey.

Contents

Preface

Getting out of do-do.

I am not kidding. This book is all about getting out of do-do!

"Do-do" is the mode in which most businesspeople seem to always be stuck. Head down, shoulder to the wheel, nose to the grindstone, push, push, push. We are always doing. Maybe it makes us feel better. Maybe it is an animal instinct that comes from ancient history. Wherever it came from, it can be expensive, less productive than we think, and can make us downright ineffective.

It is easy to fool ourselves when we are hard at "do-do" work. That is why it is often called busywork. We look busy. That gets us promoted. We work extra hours. We complain that we cannot get away from our desks. We always seem to be in "do-do" mode.

What is important is to get out of the "do-do" trap and instead strive for "done-done." It is important to do work; it is more important to get work done. Finish something. Get results. Move forward.

That is what this book is all about. Find the places in your organization where there is just too much "do-do." You can find them in any operation, whether it's a not-for-profit, a manufacturer, or even a hobby. The most successful people and the most profitable businesses (other than the government) are always finishing things. They operate, live in, and encourage "done-done."

One old saying that fits is: "The good is the enemy of the best." How often will we keep tweaking something to try to make it just a little bit better, or even perfect? Instead, we should get to the point where it is functional and get it out the door.

We can make more progress if we get a product or service in the hands of a customer. Let them tell you what needs to be fixed. If they are happy, you can be happy.

Sometimes we just need to test our assumptions. Try a small test sample. Be prepared to pull your new product or service back in. Learn from the market. Make adjustments and try it again; get more feedback and keep working at it until the market says you are ready for prime time.

Be fast, get things done, but do not accept sloppy work. Poor quality will hurt you every time. *But,* good quality work that gets the job done is usually much faster to market, less expensive to build (or to do in the case of services), satisfies the customer, and builds a strong "done-done" reputation.

Another common expression and consequence of "do-do" is "paralysis by analysis." We have all seen companies that miss opportunities because they study them to death. They are worried they might miss something. They are afraid of being wrong (see page 113 for a short discussion of why we are so afraid of being wrong).

In our modern world, *action trumps everything* (this is the title of a book by Leonard A. Schlesinger, Charles F. Kiefer, and Paul B. Brown; I met Len while participating in a special program for entrepreneurship educators at Babson College). We need to keep moving forward. We need to take action to get things done.

Concepts like rapid prototyping and increasing the velocity of failure are the keys to a successful future. We need to try things, learn from the experience, correct our course, and try again. In this book, you will find many examples of times when ideas were perfected by trial and error. No one was penalized. Instead, they were rewarded. They were rewarded with ultimate success, better processes, and environments in which continuous improvement is the priority.

Some people will say, "But that is not our culture." I respectfully disagree. Culture should not be used as an excuse for not doing the right thing. Culture is the glue that holds groups together. Do not confuse culture with bad habits. Get out of the "do-do" bad habits and move into the profitability of "done-done."

In this book, we will examine ways to get to "done-done" by asking simple questions to diagnose opportunities and focus on solutions; then, we will come up with something to try and put it into action. We will use results to evaluate how well our first idea worked, and then we will improve on it.

Because this is a long-term process, we can make improvements at any time—on the spur of the moment or over long stretches of time. Every process can be improved. So pick the low-hanging fruit, get some benefits, and spread the process to every part of the operation.

There is plenty of opportunity to improve. Stop thinking about it and get something done. You will be amazed at how much you can accomplish.

Acknowledgments

I want to recognize Clint Greenleaf, who saw the value of this book while I was working with his organization. He believed the general business reader could use these ideas to improve everything they do. The fact that we were being hit with one of the most severe economic downturns in history increased the urgency to get this book out. Without his help, it might still be sitting in my head and only a few companies would be able to gain from these insights.

I would like to thank Jeff Gusdorf, who has taken my place running the Brown Smith Wallace Consulting Group. He has given me ideas, perspective, and encouragement.

Finally, special thanks goes to Louise, my best friend and harshest critic since 1967. She has kept me honest and challenged me to stay on track.

How This Book Is Organized

It is true that you only have to start the process and then get out of the way! But, how do you do that? Be prepared to be surprised. This book's organization is as simple as one, two, three—one *goal*, two *questions*, and three *principles*.

SECTION I: THE ONE GOAL

The process of improvement begins by examining your own reasons to exist and establishing a primary goal for your organization. By providing a documented goal or objectives, you make it easier for others to help generate the results that you want, whether these are more profits, a better lifestyle, positive impact on your community, or whatever else you might aspire to.

SECTION II: THE TWO QUESTIONS

There are only two questions that you really need to ask. These questions are the keys to becoming effective in what you do. They will help you focus on the "do-do" in your operation. Use the input from their answers to move your organization to "done-done." They represent the quickest way to find opportunities that can improve everything an organization does. The questions may seem simple, but their success has been proven by more than forty years of field testing.

Learn how to use these questions effectively and there will be no limits to what you can do. Teach them to managers and staff. Encourage everyone to use them on a regular basis. You will find that amazing improvements are possible at every level of the organization.

To help you understand exactly what you are capable of achieving, this second section is filled with stories from over forty years of experience working in the field. I hope these stories will encourage you and spark ideas as you work to improve operations in your own company. They will help you see how truly easy it is to find opportunities and take advantage of them.

These stories come from all types of organizations, from small not-for-profits to large, multinational operations. Manufacturers, distributors, retailers, and service organizations are all represented. Use them as examples for your teams. You may even find some that sound familiar. Many businesses do the same types of things. Take the lessons of others and apply them to your own organization. It will help get the ball rolling.

Some stories may seem out of date (for example, early adopters of fax machines and experimentation with electronic phone systems), but they are instructive. Think about the "guts" it took to suggest some of the ideas. Would you have done it? Could you have predicted the success? Does it seem so obvious now? What are similar ideas or situations you are facing right now? The technology may be different, but the environment could be exactly the same. Substitute e-mail for fax or social networking for the electronic phone system.

If you have an interesting, unusual, or just fun situation you would like to share, we are all ears. There will be an online database of ideas and actions that others have found and successfully implemented. Send your examples to me at: Steve@SteveEpner.com. Then follow the new stories being posted at SteveEpner.com.

SECTION III: THE THREE PRINCIPLES

This section shares three principles that will guide you as you implement changes based on the answers you get to the two questions.

These principles will help you focus on and accept the best new ideas, implement change, and focus your energies.

You will learn to keep things short and simple, that it is okay to be wrong, and that everything we do should add value. Put this all together and it becomes easier to understand why we need to be effective, not just efficient.

By setting goals, asking questions, and following simple principles, it is possible to achieve extraordinary results. You will be able to improve outcomes, keep your employees engaged, and have a better day-to-day experience. It all goes back to getting out of do-do and getting to done-done!

EXTRAS

In this final section of the book, I have included material that should be of help when executing the ideas presented in each previous section. It starts with a chapter on the details of holding a meeting: how to determine the location, time, and room setup, along with other pointers to help make any meeting more successful.

Second is a short discussion of the "opportunity in the ordinary." All around us are opportunities that most people ignore; they do not even recognize their existence.

Lastly, I've included a short section for employees on how to prepare new ideas for presentation to their boss or innovation committee. My goal is to help more ideas make it out of the brain and onto the table where action can be taken.

ONE LAST COMMENT

In a done-done world, it is okay to start where you want and then skip around. Some people might want to start with the three principles first. The principles will give them a foundation and focus for their efforts. They may help some people avoid that horrible "paralysis by analysis" roadblock that halts so many good ideas.

Others will want to start with the questions and stories. These will give them ideas that can be applied to their own organizations. Staff people may choose to start at the end, with the chapter on how to present an idea.

And, if you like to start at the beginning of a book and work through it in order, that is also perfect. In a done-done world, there is rarely only one right way to do anything. Wherever you start is the right place.

It may be a trite old saying, but the good is the enemy of the best. Just start reading, thinking, and getting things done. Get to a point where you have read enough to be confident and then try something. You will keep improving as you go. At every opportunity, you can make things better. More important, you will start seeing results. That is one of the wonderful things about a done-done world.

SECTION I
The One Goal

SECTION I

The One Goal

There is only one overriding goal and that is to *improve the way your business operates.* We have to find ways to get out of the do-do mode and into the done-done world of achievement.

How this goal is realized may differ by organization. The common requirement is an open, safe environment. If the employees feel threatened, they will not cooperate or contribute. Keep this in mind as you plan every action associated with the concepts in this book.

Every idea in this book is focused on improvement. How you implement them will be affected by the personality of your organization. Some people will start small, almost invisibly. Others will make a splash. Go for the method that feels most comfortable.

Keep focused on the goal and the results will take care of themselves. Your first outcome will be better processes and a generally improved atmosphere. After that, it only gets better: greater profits, better customer experiences, and much more are just waiting to be found. Trust your people and yourself. As the process starts to deliver results, you will be glad you did.

CHAPTER 1

The Basic Idea

It seemed an insurmountable problem. Sales had been going up, but they had leveled off and profits were dropping. Something was wrong, but what was it? Management was stuck. They had tried a number of different things, but nothing seemed to work. Then, in one of those amazing coincidences, a supervisor overheard part of a conversation and made an offhand remark about how the staff had always wondered why a certain process had been instituted. It slowed everything down, discouraged the inside sales force, and caused more problems than it was intended to solve.

Luckily, the supervisor who heard the remark did not ignore what the line person said, but thought through the issue and realized the process was robbing profits from the whole company. He quickly met with the top management. In this meeting, he explained what was happening and what it was costing.

It turned out the process had been added to resolve a pet peeve of one of the top executives. It took guts, but the supervisor decided to pursue the company's need to unravel the process, to simplify it. Understanding the politics, he came up with a new method of correcting the situation. He added metrics to show what it was costing and the savings that could be realized with the proposed change. He sold it to the executives and received permission to implement the change.

It worked. The time from order entry to cash was reduced. Removing this one irritant did not turn the whole company around, but the attitudes of the sales team improved. In return, the customer experience improved and a small (but significant) increase in sales was noted. More important, the overall cost of doing business was reduced and the first hints of profits began to return, even on lower sales dollars.

The best result was that the supervisor rewarded the employee who had pointed out the problem. The employee was asked to help define how he would resolve the issue. Then the supervisor established a program to encourage more input. Tentatively at first, staff members came forward with observations of things that did not seem right. Now improvements were being made on a regular basis. Every success encouraged others to come forward. The company became much more profitable, gained market share, and created a workforce that was invested in its future, not just a weekly paycheck.

Is this an extreme example? Maybe. But there are similar stories throughout the business world and opportunities in each of our organizations.

This book is dedicated to finding the gems of ideas hidden away in the minds of our staff members. They really *are* capable of improving our operations—even if they do not have a Harvard MBA. All we need to do is encourage them to offer ideas and reward them when those ideas work. It is that simple.

Simple is the key word. In section III, there is a whole chapter on keeping it simple ("KISS Is Not Stupid"). Management can always make things complicated. Sometimes all we have to do is simplify a process. It gets us to "done" faster, with less effort and usually with better results.

The concepts and details described in this book are based on over forty years of helping companies find new answers to old questions. Some refer to this as innovating, or finding a new path. People call it breaking paradigms and all kinds of other names.

The most important thing to remember is that the world is changing around us. It is not static; instead, it is in constant motion. As such, it is up to us to choose how to react when change occurs. We can choose to react with fear or with purpose.

The ideas, methods, and processes that follow will help you find ways to improve everything you do. Many times companies have the answers right in front of them but are blind to the information. However, every organization has people who really know how the work gets done and understand what is needed to succeed.

Any operation can take advantage of the tremendous intelligence hiding in their staff. All too often, companies ignore this important and cost-effective consulting tool.

As you read ahead, you will find an easy-to-follow method that will help improve the operations of your organization—for profit or not-for-profit. You will find easy ways to increase accuracy (doing things right the first time to avoid doing them over), reduce procedures (stop doing things that are unnecessary—mostly do-do work), and work smarter (get things done in less time with fewer resources).

Everyone will learn to focus on the ultimate customer, eliminating tasks that do not add value. Service will improve as you concentrate on what is important.

I have been teaching these methods for many years and never cease to be amazed at what staff and supervisors come up with at every level of the organization. Sometimes the path to growth just involves being willing to change a viewpoint, being willing to listen to someone else (internal and external), or just being unafraid to challenge the status quo. In other cases, research and experimentation are necessary. In every situation, the results are impressive.

I teach the process to the students in the Saint Louis University MBA program. For their semester project in my corporate entrepreneurship class, each student must develop and propose an idea that will improve the operation at his or her current employer's company. Plus, the proposed idea must return a benefit at least equal to the cost of the student's education (at the time of writing, just over $50,000 for the one-year MBA).

The results are amazing. It works. Every student finds opportunities that can easily pay for his or her education. All it takes is a bit of encouragement, some support, and a willingness to consider new ideas.

It is wonderful to read the ideas the students find, and the companies that are willing to implement these ideas gain tremendous benefits. In too many operations, so many good ideas are lost or not even suggested. In this book, you will learn how to encourage employees to expose the obvious, but hidden, possibilities that can eliminate all kinds of waste and operational roadblocks.

Try an experiment. Test some of the ideas on a small select group. Learn what is possible. Then take the ideas to the whole organization. The end results will be worth the effort.

CHAPTER 2

Why We Ignore Good Input

Your people are a repository of information that is rarely tapped. They know answers that can be used to solve—or at least make positive progress on—the big problems your organization is facing. Start by asking yourself, "Why are employees reluctant to tell the boss what can be done? And why are so many suggestions ignored?"

There are three major reasons why top management does not get the data, knowledge, and wisdom that are locked in the minds of the company's most important assets—its employees:

- Most never ask,
- When they do ask, most never listen, and
- Even when they ask *and* listen, most do not trust their employees' perceptions, so they do nothing with the knowledge.

Why? To begin with, too many executives and senior managers feel that they should already know the answers—all the answers. Many worry that admitting they could use help will be perceived as a sign of weakness or even incompetence in the organizational culture.

Instead of asking for help from those who might know the answers, they think, "If I read the right management book and go to enough seminars, I will learn what I need to know. There are so many new things to try. One of them has to work . . . right?"

Worse, there are times when members of senior management do ask for help, but they are not sincere. Sometimes, they go through the motions just to get "buy in." They may be hoping that a combination of the latest managerial fad with some employee participation will generate a quick and easy fix.

They may even ask the right questions, but it is obvious they are not interested in any answers that come from the staff. Even when they do listen, key points are ignored because of management's preconceived notions about the way things are or should be.

It is also obvious that many top managers do not trust the answers that come from the staff. It is as though they are thinking: "How could 'one of them' know what to do when I don't?" They may be afraid of failure (what if the idea sounds good but ultimately does not work?) or just the unknown (no one else has proved this is a correct answer; I am not ready to go out on a limb for something new). They do not have confidence in the staff (or maybe themselves), and it shows.

There are many great business stories about how companies ignored the advice or ideas of their staff. Kodak could have had the first digital camera (they did get the patent), but they could not see photography without film. The Kodak executives did not understand the new product their development group had designed. If they had only paid attention, you would probably not be reading about Kodak filing for bankruptcy.

VisiCalc (for those old enough to remember the name) owned the spreadsheet market, but Lotus 1-2-3 eclipsed them and then lost out to Excel. How many internal people had ideas that would have kept VisiCalc at the forefront? No one will ever know for sure, but my bet is there were many good ideas ignored because they did not fit the mold.

Then there are the many stories about Ross Perot and IBM. In one, he exceeded his annual sales quota by the end of January. When he proposed his innovative strategies to his supervisors, they disregarded him. So he quit and started his own company. By most accounts, he is one of the one hundred richest men in America. IBM has not done poorly (although they did have some major ups and downs), but where might they be today if they had listened to Ross and kept him on board?

The business landscape is littered with similar stories. Stop and think. What new ideas have your people brought you that you have ignored? What is on your desk today that could ensure the future of your company for years, but is not even being considered?

There is a solution, but it is one that takes courage and belief in your people before you can even be ready to contemplate the possibilities. Strong, self-confident managers, combined with leaders who are willing to listen and are able to trust their people, can always harvest the knowledge base within any organization. More important, the benefits of that harvest will be both immediate and long lasting.

If you have the self-confidence to "let your people go," if your ego can accept the concept that you do not have and need not have all the answers, and if you are willing to believe in your people and try a new process, then you will find that the ideas in this book can unleash incredible power. Your organization will benefit immensely from the knowledge, passion, enthusiasm, and caring that has been locked inside your people for far too long.

CHAPTER 3

Setting Objectives

Defining the objectives for any organization takes time and effort. You can do this at the same time you start asking the questions that will reveal the opportunities that are available. The organization's specific strategic goals and underlying objectives become the filter through which various options and opportunities are passed. Not every idea is worth the investment of time and effort (or another idea may just be more important). Having a filter that helps you recognize what you should be doing and let go of the rest is of prime importance to your success.

In the classic story *Alice in Wonderland*, Alice arrives at a fork in the road. She asks the Cheshire Cat in a tree which way she should go. The cat asks her where she wants to go, and Alice answers, "I do not know."

"Then," says the cat, "it doesn't much matter which way you go, does it?"

It is the same with our desire to improve "things." If we do not know what is important to achieve, then it does not much matter what we try to get done or how we do it.

Management needs to provide two pieces of input to the staff. The first is an understanding of the business they are in (see page 15), and the second is a definition of the large objectives for the organization's program. It can be as simple as "improve profits" or "reduce processing time." It might be as specific as "increase referrals from existing customers" or "boost gross margin in a specific line." Pick any one of your objectives as your primary target and then let your staff and mangers loose.

One key to achieving objectives is being able to recognize success. There is an old management saying that is very true and fits here: "If you cannot measure it, you cannot manage it." Whatever targets you set as part of your objectives, it is important to know what is to be measured, how it will be measured, where you are today, and where you want to be. (Please see chapter 5, "Developing Metrics," starting on page 19.)

Complete the process by determining what resources are available to help get you there and identifying a champion to lead the charge. This is described in more detail in the chapters "Simplified Project Planning" (page 23) and "Implementing Change" (page 71).

Before moving on, list a few of the big-picture results that you hope to accomplish in your organization. Let those items help you see the possibilities.

_____

_____

_____

_____

_____

_____

_____

_____

CHAPTER 4

What Business Are We In?

Strategic planning and corporate goal setting are mostly outside the realm of this book. However, a few brief notes are important. As mentioned earlier, goals are a filter though which all new ideas can be passed. If an idea supports the goal, it is one to consider. If it does not, leave it for another time. We suggest setting up an "idea parking lot" to capture all of the good ideas that come up. While every idea may not be the right thing to work on today, it may be very worthwhile later on. Come back to the idea parking lot frequently to get inspiration and new things to work on.

In the corporate entrepreneurship class at Saint Louis University, one of the first lessons and homework assignments has to do with determining what business a company is in. Back in 1960, the *Harvard Business Review* published a famous article by Theodore Levitt titled "Marketing Myopia." Levitt made the point that if the railroads had been in the transportation business rather than the railroad business, they would have owned the airlines.

Today, some might argue that the railroads were lucky not to own the airlines. From a different perspective, what if they had seen the future and become transportation experts? Would we have a better model? Maybe the United States would have a better-integrated travel grid with short-run, high-speed railroads connecting long-haul air hubs. No one knows the answer for sure, but the potential was there, even though no one realized it at the time.

Thomas Winninger tells a similar story about Hertz. The company believed they were in the car rental business. This meant that they competed on exactly the same basis as everyone else in the auto-rental industry. There was no differentiation. Every car rental company looked about the same. Price was a major consideration. Sometimes the types of cars for rent were different or there might be more choices, but there was little real differentiation.

With a bit of work, some open-mindedness, and a lot of discussion, the Hertz executives figured out they should be in the "Get out of the airport quick" business. All of a sudden, they changed the mode and focus of everything they did.

The Hertz #1 Club Gold allowed frequent renters to skip the rental counter (remember the long, *slow* lines waiting for dot-matrix printers to bang out four-part contracts?) and go directly to their car in the lot. The keys were in the ignition, the rental contract was hanging from the mirror, and all renters had to do was show their driver's license to the guard on the way out of the lot.

Many business travelers were happy to pay extra dollars every day to get out of the airport fast. Of course, the idea was so good and so successful that all of the other rental companies followed suit with programs of their own. Still, Hertz got the jump-start and accumulated market share while waiting for the others to figure out what was most important to the customer.

Ask yourself, "What business should we really be in?" The answer will provide a way to evaluate new ideas. Do they support your business? Do they help you do a better job in the marketplace?

Play with this question. It can offer you great insight into the market and your customers. What do they really want? Interview your best customers, the largest and the smallest. Talk to past customers and find out why they left. You may be missing opportunities that are obvious to others.

Another way to find strategies to lead your market space is to ask, "What could we do that would change the way the industry works?" Do not allow yourself to be limited by technology, investment capital, or time. Reality will come later. The first step is to find the seemingly invisible opportunities that will allow you to change the way the world perceives you and your abilities.

It is possible to become the dominant player by changing the rules. Apple did not invent the cell phone; they just changed the rules concerning what a cell phone looked like and how it worked.

Some changes are easy—they are just a change in the market perception of you and your brand. Long before Kodak missed the boat on digital photography, they ran up against Fujifilm. Market share kept eroding. Then they changed the marketing message from selling film to selling memories. Consumers were asked, "Whom would you trust with your memories?" That question hit a chord with the American public and Kodak was able to regain sales and customers.

There are many dramatic examples of companies that failed to make the necessary changes in their market. Sometimes this resistance to growth has been disastrous, such as with the typewriter companies that could not imagine word processors becoming something everyone wanted and could afford. They believed that word processing would never replace a good electric typewriter.

Then there are many bookstores (which I miss) that did not believe online sales would ever suffice for the dedicated reader who came in to browse books before they purchased them. These are just two simple examples. As you can imagine, there are many more.

What is happening in your industry? What new forces are going to affect the way you do business? What are young executives and line people talking about? How are their habits changing?

Find out what the "weird" people are doing. Think hard about the ideas that supposedly "just won't work" (for instance, word processors replacing typewriters or cassette tapes replacing records, only to be replaced by CDs and then memory chips in electronic players). Consider far-out ideas carefully. It is possible that some people have already seen the future. Learn from them and experiment on your own.

What is possible (or impossible) today that could suddenly and completely change the markets you know so well? This is a critical question and you need to explore the potential answers. If you are prepared for the future, you can conquer it. Otherwise, it may conquer you!

Take some time to make notes about what business you are in and what business you should be in. It will make a big difference in how you approach new ideas.

_____

_____

_____

_____

_____

_____

_____

_____

CHAPTER 5

Developing Metrics

It is extremely important to know how you will recognize success. The old excuse "I will know it when I see it" will not work. Results must be measurable, traceable, and agreed upon. This encourages teamwork and focused projects. A lack of objective measures will dilute your efforts. If everyone has a different sense of what the end result should be, they will end up working at cross purposes to one another. Then you are stuck back in that "do-do" world we want to eliminate.

No matter how well you define your goals, without metrics the potential for success is severely limited. Each goal needs to be measurable. Then it is possible to manage a team to accomplish the goals set by the organization's leadership.

As a short aside, it is important to understand the difference between leaders and managers (which is not as easy as it seems). Leaders set the goals, and managers implement them. That is not to say that there is never any overlap, only that each group has their own specific requirements. Excellent leaders may not be good managers and that is okay. Good managers can become superior leaders, but their management capabilities are necessary to succeed at converting goals into reality.

The foundation of management is very simple. Managers get

paid for one thing and one thing only. They get paid to move numbers. Leaders are rewarded for setting strategic directions that generate better-than-average returns. The best leaders find the right numbers to be moved, decide which direction to move the numbers, how far to move them, and how much to invest in moving them, and establish time frames in which to accomplish the goals. Then they hire the best managers to accomplish their vision.

That is an MBA in a paragraph. So what does all this really mean and how can it be used?

As we already discussed, "You can only manage what you can measure." The concept is very simple. Anything that cannot be measured cannot be managed because we have no way to know if we are doing a good job or not. Poor managers will tell you, "What I do cannot be measured, but you will know it when you see it." Do not believe it. In almost forty years in business, I have never found one worthwhile goal that could not be measured. I am ready to be corrected, but am confident there will be few if any contenders.

An easy example to consider is customer satisfaction. It is not on the balance sheet, it cannot be found on the profit and loss statement, and usually, it is not even tracked. So how can we measure something as vague as customer satisfaction?

This is where leadership comes in. Every company needs to be led. Every good idea needs a leader and a champion or a manager.

Good leaders have clear visions of where they want to go. The best are able to sell their visions to others and then reduce those visions to measurable goals. They can articulate what they expect in clearly defined terms that are easy to monitor.

For example, customer service might be measured by the number of referrals given by existing customers. The more satisfied our customers are, the more referrals they will give us.

We might use surveys to find out what our customers think. Just be careful not to fool yourself. A poorly worded survey sent to the wrong group can make you feel good . . . while the world is crashing down around you. If you want to use a survey, get a professional group to administer it. Survey a mix of current and past customers. Find out why they stay or why they left. Make sure your data is statistically accurate. This tool can help you learn a great deal about the level of satisfaction you are delivering.

A survey is not a one-time event. It must be an ongoing process. Unless you are developing and reporting results on a regular basis, a survey will have a very limited impact on the business. What you need is a consistent set of numbers that can be used to present results in an easy-to-understand manner. You and your people need to watch the numbers and know that they are moving in the right direction and at the right velocity.

This consistent monitoring will put you in a position to develop metrics that can be used to make sure customer service is improving—or tell you point-blank that you need to change what you are doing because the numbers aren't good. If the survey metrics are getting worse, it is time to do something different. Take advantage of your knowledge of what is really happening to improve the situation. Ignore reality at your own peril.

There are many more ways to measure customer satisfaction, but the most important thing to recognize is that it can be measured in the first place. Once we accept that anything important can be measured, coming up with the method is relatively easy.

Take your time; make sure you know how the measurement will work. Experiment and challenge your initial results. Having the correct measurement is extremely important. If you don't create an accurate metric, you might accidentally spend a great deal of time and energy moving in the wrong direction.

It is also important that the rest of the team understands and believes in the metric. They are the ones who will ultimately succeed or fail based on the results that are reported.

Allow the team champion (manager) to participate in the development of the metric and validate that it will reflect reality. This manager should also approve the resources and targets (see the next section on project planning and management).

Before leaving this page, consider spending just a few minutes thinking about the importance of measurement in your organization. Jot down some notes about what metrics would accurately reflect the status of your big ideas.

_____

_____

_____

_____

_____

_____

_____

_____

CHAPTER 6

Simplified Project Planning

Your final step before turning over the opportunities you find to managers is to build upon the metrics defined in the previous chapter. You must identify two positioning points and select a champion who will work with the leadership to establish *short-term* deliverables. This is the foundation of project planning and management. It will help you succeed and get to done-done more quickly and easily.

To start, you must carefully define how to calculate the metrics already identified. The team must believe it is a reasonable metric that will accurately reflect progress. Next (and this may seem obvious—but it's not), share the data and your analysis with your managers. Show them all the calculations that will be used to perform the measurements. Get their reactions and input. If they are comfortable with what you are asking, there is greater potential for success. Remember, they are betting their futures on the accuracy of the metrics, and in turn, on the success of your organization. Without the proper understanding, they will be unable to move the numbers.

Then come the two points. It is critical to know where you are and where you want to be. Where you are is the baseline, the starting point. It may take time to actually calculate the numbers, but it is important that the manager and everyone on the team accept the initial measurement.

Once there is a baseline, then it is possible to determine where you want to be. If, for example, you are measuring errors in shipment picking, you might want to reach zero errors; just be careful you do not choose an impossible target. That will discourage people, not energize them. Be realistic. Do your homework. Find out what the best companies in your industry, geographic area, or size group are doing. It will be a good starting target and will get the team moving forward.

Next, you need a champion or manager. We will use the titles interchangeably in this context. Success requires someone who is passionate about the project and the opportunity it presents. That person will have to rally resources, fight roadblocks, change perceptions, and manage a team. If the champion does not believe in what he or she is doing, these things cannot be done well.

If you can't find a champion, you may have the wrong project—or in some extreme cases, the wrong people in your organization. Either recruit a champion or move to another opportunity. The basic problems will stick around. Demonstrate progress, fix things, reward people, and it will become easier to find the champions for those more difficult but extremely worthwhile projects.

Given the expected results, work with the project champion to determine a time frame to get there. Be realistic. Make sure you give the champion and his or her teams time, resources, and support to meet the goals. Setting anyone up for failure will have a negative effect on the company as a whole.

The champion should participate in setting the time frame expectations based on the resource allocation. If management wishes for a shorter time frame, then they must negotiate with the champion and either provide more resources or change the expectations. Due dates cannot be forced. If they are, then the project is a failure before it starts.

If the executives do not like the answer that the champion proposes, and they do not believe there are additional resources or do not want to reduce expectations, then they can look for a different champion who believes he or she can meet the objective with the available resources.

Just do not force someone to pick up the project and champion it if he or she doesn't believe in it. That will cause many problems down the road and destroy the sense of trust that you need for your organization to realize the greatest returns for continuing efforts.

One other suggestion is to keep task definitions short and simple. It is much easier to get your hands around a one-week project than a one-year project. Shorter time frames insure a greater likelihood of success. Making it easy for people to succeed is very valuable when beginning this process. Remember, success breeds success. Do everything possible to make sure there are more successes than failures.

With every measurable activity, there needs to be frequent reporting. The proper schedule will depend on the organization, the metrics, and the potential response time.

The concept of "responsibility reports" works well. The managers are given access to all of the data that they can control and receive reports on the results of their efforts. This is what they need to manage.

Finally, it is important to plan and distribute rewards for the teams and groups that reach their measurable goals in the requested time. Every success should be celebrated.

Every publicized success will make the next one easier. Rewards can run the gamut from simple public recognition to monetary rewards based on delivered results. Publicize the rewards and the recipient's reactions. This is a great way to build momentum. It will encourage others to try—and that is worth a fortune.

SECTION II
The Two Questions

SECTION II

The Two Questions

Since starting my consulting firm in 1976, I have learned that there are two key questions that can unlock the knowledge that is waiting to be discovered:

- What is the dumbest thing your company is doing?
- What is the most difficult or most time-consuming thing your company is doing?

Once you open these doors, the company will be able to take advantage of amazing insights and great ideas.

As I pointed out in section I, line people know the answers to the most burning questions about processes and procedures. As owners and managers, you must be willing to listen, to accept that others may have good ideas, and to admit that you might be wrong (or are not the most knowledgeable person in the company). If you accept these basic premises, then asking these two simple questions, listening carefully to the answers, and taking action based on what you learn will help you gain competitive advantage in your market, business, and industry.

In the following chapters, I will introduce the two questions and provide a number of real-life examples to help you understand how to gain the greatest advantage from the answers.

For both questions, be willing to look beyond the superficial to the underlying problems. It is too easy to work on symptoms of problems. They are easy to spot and band-aids already exist for most. These bandages will hide—and even cure—the symptoms. But the big problems will not go away. They will continue to spawn new symptoms until the real problems are dealt with directly.

CHAPTER 7

Questioning

I often suggest asking "why" five times to attempt to diagnose any situation. One company called me in to design a new hiring system for them. Their turnover had increased and it was taking too much time to process all of the paper work.

My first question was, "Why?" and they responded that because of the turnover, the volume of persons needing to be hired had increased and they could not keep up with the paperwork.

My second question was, "Why?" and they just stared at me. So, I asked, "Why do you have so much turnover?" After a few seconds and very confused looks, one person hesitantly answered, "Because people quit?"

"No," I explained. "What I want to know is, why are all of those people quitting?"

They did not have an answer. So we had to do some research. It turned out that the company was paying significantly below scale for the area. Their approach had been to hire the chronically unemployed, then teach them a skill and how to show up for work every day. As soon as they became good employees, the employee could leave and get a 10 percent raise anywhere else in town.

My suggestion was that instead of designing a new system, they just needed to increase what they were paying people. I might as well have suggested that they try to send a man to the moon. The first and second reactions were, "We cannot afford that," and, "It would not fit our pay-scale document." At this point, I asked my favorite question again: "Why?"

Once the research was completed and the client could see the real cost of hiring, training, and replacing employees, the cost of increasing salaries seemed like a bargain. Of course, they did not have to pay out the complete raise all at once. They still hired persons at below-scale salaries, but used the extra money to provide one or more merit raises as the new employees gained skills and perfect time and attendance records. By the end of the first full year, they were just about equal to everyone else in town, but the merit raises made them feel much better about the company and turnover almost ceased.

I could have charged them a nice fee to design a hiring system, but that would have been the wrong answer. It would have simply covered up a symptom of the problem. The underlying problem would have remained and been a drag on the company's profitability. By asking "why," we were able to identify the real issue and correct it. That made all of the difference in the world.

Each of the two questions is, in itself, a complete diagnostic. The answers they generate will highlight opportunities in every part of the organization. They will get your people engaged in improving things. Together, they will provide you with tens of thousands of dollars' worth of free consulting that is focused on your specific needs.

When you are ready to get started, give all participating staff people a small spiral notebook to keep in their shirt pocket or purse. Ask them to write notes and answers to the two questions every time they see something in the company's operations that they find "dumb," difficult, or time-consuming. Tell them not to hope they remember. They need to take action and write it down as soon as they can.

Get yourself a spiral notebook and set a great example.

CHAPTER 8

Question One

The first question can be asked in many different ways. Each way should try to get the staff personnel to have some fun taking a hard look at what is going on in the company. Here are a few possibilities for question one:

- What is the dumbest thing we make you do?
- What is the dumbest thing you did today?
- What is the dumbest thing you have seen someone doing?

This question, in all of its forms, works for a number of different reasons. First of all, any question helps to focus our attention. Without some direction or focus, our minds wander. Sometimes that wandering is what we want and need (especially if we are working on innovating new ideas, products, or strategies). When the goal is to find better ways to do something or everything, the correct question will get us on the right track.

Using a question like "What is the dumbest . . ." does more than just focus the mind on the issue at hand (every dumb thing represents an opportunity to improve). It tells the audience that asking questions is not intimidating. It can be fun. Relax, and we can all laugh at ourselves. Of course, if top management then gets defensive or immediately finds excuses (especially if they are overly invested in the activity being discussed), the staff will quickly believe this is a trick question that will only hurt them if they answer honestly.

This question works best if everyone in management understands the stakes and makes clear their support for the goal of the process—finding opportunities to improve. They must be willing to admit they might have been wrong when they originally instituted a policy or procedure. They have to be ready to admit they may not have seen an obvious problem. They have to be ready to fess up to the group that they do not know every answer to every question. Every person has to be willing to step back and consider any input, no matter where it comes from. Encouraging the staff will pay big dividends, and asking the right questions will provide the best answers.

Go ahead, try it yourself. Start with the first thing(s) that happened this morning. What was the first interruption to your day? Was it a fax? Maybe you got hung up on e-mail messages. Was there an activity you needed to approve, but after consideration, you realized you hadn't rejected any submitted paperwork in years? All of these incidents might lead to your awareness of a dumb thing.

Take the fax. Why was it delivered to you? Could someone down the line have handled it? What if you did not take care of it? What negative effects would occur? If the answer is none, then you have stumbled on a dumb thing that could be fixed.

How about e-mail? Are you copied on too many messages? Most managers get way too many e-mails. They are sent by subordinates who are just playing CYA based on past experience. What if you started a new policy? People who send you a copy of an e-mail will have to meet with you to explain why they sent it and what action they expected you to take.

If it is just CYA, firmly tell them you will accept a summary of what was decided upon and the final actions taken when the project is completed. You do not want to be included unless your input is required. If it isn't, they need to take you out of the loop.

In this case, you can set a goal of reducing your e-mail traffic by 50 percent. If this scares you, then we have found another problem. It may be that you do not have the right people working for you because you do not trust them to do the right thing. Or maybe you have never trained your staff to do the work correctly.

Today I hear many people tell me that, with staff reductions, there is no one else to handle all the details. Regardless, this is something you can work on correcting in the short term because it will free you up in the long term. I have never found anyone who requires all the e-mail they get. Take a long and hard look at what you are receiving. Get rid of what you really do not need.

If you are receiving e-mails to review an activity or give approval to proceed, track the number of acceptances and rejections over a week or a month. If there are no rejections, quickly get out of the checking business. If there are lots of rejections, it is time to better train your staff or change the process.

In one situation at a larger company, the CFO was approving every payment. That was the way it had always been done. After a short review, it was determined that there were never any rejections for amounts under $500. That became the first threshold for review. By the end of six months, the amount had been raised to $5,000 and the CFO reclaimed at least an hour a day.

This was valuable time. The CFO's actions also sent an important message of trust to the controller and the rest of the financial services staff, giving them a greater sense of importance and responsibility. The process of approving and issuing checks was better managed because the controller was interested in proving that the CFO was right to trust his decision-making abilities. If there ever was a question, he would bring it to her on an exception basis. He took great pride in being trusted and it showed.

Next, think about something else you see every day that often causes you to ask, "Why?" It might be that the receptionist does not unlock the front door until exactly 8:00 a.m., even if customers are waiting to be served.

We have all had negative feelings about a service organization that makes us wait simply because that is the rule. What if we opened the doors fifteen minutes early? What would that cost and what benefits might it have?

One of our clients (a construction supply company) started opening at 6:30 a.m. instead of 7:00 a.m. like the competition. They found that some customers arrived even earlier because it helped them get their day started on time. Providing free coffee and donuts helped increase traffic (yes, there were some freeloaders, but they were a small minority) and sales increased significantly more than the nominal cost for food. There was no extra salary cost because the two guys who opened early were allowed to leave thirty minutes earlier—and they loved it. There were a few more interruptions during the first shift, but staff quickly figured out how to handle the traffic without impacting the rest of the operation.

The next question they needed to ask was, what happens if a customer arrives even earlier? The answer was to set up a small entry area that was opened when the first employee arrived. They set out coffee for the early birds and added the donuts as soon as they were delivered. Their operation became the favorite gathering place for construction workers in the area. A significant side benefit was the amount of market intelligence that was learned by listening to the workers' conversations.

The word spread, and soon this company was where everyone in the industry congregated (even if they did not need something) to get the inside news on what was happening. It became a real competitive advantage. The outside sales guys took turns coming in early to listen to the word on the street. It gave them better intelligence about what work was coming long before public announcements were made. They got a real leg up on the competition by finding out about many projects first. Sure, it started out as a reaction to a stupid thing (not opening the doors when a customer showed up before the official starting time), but it paid off big.

In the examples that follow are a few answers to question one to get your mental juices flowing. Think about how simple they are. Find examples in your workplace. You will be surprised at how easy this process can be.

Time to start: Use your notebook to find at least one thing that might be considered dumb before moving on. If you are stuck, just ask some of the line people. If they trust you, they will give you lots of ammunition.

Answer: Our sales commission structure is so complicated. It is different for each salesperson and sometimes even by customer.

What was done? This company was not alone in identifying this problem. The issue comes up almost every time there is a commissioned outside sales force that has been in place more than a couple of years. Companies often tweak the commission process every time they want to change the sales force's behavior, when they want to attract a certain person, or if the owner says so; and this company was no different.

When fuel prices went sky high, commissions were reduced to make up for unrecovered local delivery charges. When a salesperson was lured away from a competitor, a special pay deal was set up. New deals were made for new products, for special customers, and in response to almost any other whim of top management.

Salespeople also made changes. They used special deals to make up for lost revenue due to the delivery surcharges. Sales management thought they were keeping the situation under control by making special deals that none of the other salespeople would know about. Of course, everyone knew about them—the guys and gals were bragging about how much they talked management out of. It became a contest to see how much extra commission could be squeezed out of every sale.

All of these special arrangements were done with the excuse that they were necessary in order to accomplish some desired end. Yet the only guarantee was that they would make paying commissions more difficult and most likely would not change any sales behaviors.

Paying commissions is a touchy subject. Salespeople seem to feel that any time a commission structure is changed, it is just to reduce their earnings. Historically, that may be correct. In order to move forward, this company needed to create a new reality. They had to simplify the commission structure to be both efficient and effective.

Research showed that many people on the sales team had become complacent and were willing to live on the fruit of previous labor. With much gnashing of teeth, screaming, and dragging of feet, some minor (major to the sales force) changes were made.

First of all, the commission structure was standardized. Special needs were handled with different draws, perks, and reimbursements. A major change was made to increase the commission value for new customers during their first year and to reduce the value for existing customers whose purchase volume did not increase beyond the value of inflation.

The company is now considering a greater change by adopting a strategic pricing model. This model is beyond the scope of this book, but it takes a strategic look at a full year's worth of sales data to identify where money is being left on the table. The results are impressive, producing additions of 2 to 4 percent of sales on the bottom line. (Please write Steve@SteveEpner.com for details on how this is done.)

Answer: We waste too much time waiting for meetings to start. Some are as much as fifteen minutes late. It seems that four to twelve people sitting around for fifteen minutes doing nothing is not a valuable use of limited resources.

What was done? At this organization, this appeared to be a growing problem, especially with regularly scheduled meetings. As a meeting got the reputation of starting late, more of the participants would arrive late so as not to waste as much of their time being unproductive.

With the approval of top management, we established a couple of new rules that seemed to solve the problem. First, if the meeting organizer did not show up within three minutes of the start time according to the synchronized clocks in every meeting room (that is another story), all of the other participants were excused to go back to work.

We asked all meeting organizers to arrive at the meeting at least five minutes early. This gave them time to talk to those who wanted to chat before the meeting began. When the start time for the meeting arrived, they were instructed to call the meeting to order, even if not everyone was there yet.

When people arrived late, they were told to just sit down and catch up. The meeting leader was not allowed to stop the meeting to fill them in on what had happened.

Plus, at the first natural break, the late attendee was penalized. In one company, anyone who is late has to tell the group a joke before the break is allowed to proceed. This seems to be sufficient punishment to eliminate most tardiness.

Once the word got out that meetings were starting on time, everyone started to show up on time. This allowed the meetings to also end punctually and saved a tremendous amount of wasted time sitting in meetings that were not productive

For the next month, keep a record of every meeting you attend. Keep score: How many started on time, how many ended on time, how many had an agenda, and how many did you really need to attend?

_____

_____

_____

_____

_____

_____

_____

_____

CHAPTER 9

Question Two

This question is an easy way to find opportunities to improve processing and the lives of your staff. Take the hard stuff and make it easier. Working with all the stakeholders on a given process will allow you to really innovate. It will enable you to find ways to simplify and improve. Here are a few possible ways to pose question two:

- What is the most difficult thing you do?
- What is the most time-consuming thing you do?

Where processes are considered difficult or time consuming, there are usually opportunities to reduce the effort required for the given set of procedures. These are chances to find more time or relieve resources to work on more important things.

Some improvements may just be in timing. For example, you might have the following simple conversation: "If we could do this in the afternoon instead of first thing in the morning, it would be much less disruptive." "No problem, there is no reason it has to be done early."

Other solutions may involve combining operations: "We do X for another department that is very similar to what we do for you. Can we consolidate the effort rather than performing two separate operations?" The best answers are something like: "If you could add ABC to the process and one extra column to the report, it would work just fine for us." Then take action: "Great, we will make the change right away."

Whenever a difficult operation is pointed out, before finding ways to simplify it, make sure it is still needed. There are many functions performed every day for some out-of-date requirement. Ask yourself and your staff if the process can be eliminated prior to spending time making it easier, faster, more accurate, or relevant.

A rule of computer science I wrote about in the late '70s stated, "If you automate garbage, all you get is faster garbage." The same is true if you improve (or enhance) "garbage" processes (ones that are not required); if you make them faster, you just end up with faster garbage. You are much better off if you can eliminate the process altogether.

Set the example. Write down at least one thing that is difficult for you to do. Then think about how it might be changed. Talk to others who are involved. You will build confidence in the process.

Answer: Every afternoon, I have to stop what I am doing to gather information from multiple sources. The report I create is very time consuming. It seems like we should be able to allow the computer to do this.

What was done? My first reaction to this issue was, "Of course, move the work to the computer and you will save a significant amount of a person's time every day." My second reaction was to make sure I understood the underlying problem rather than just papering over a symptom. So I asked why the report was being created and who used it.

The answer should not have surprised me: "I do not know." All the employee knew was that she had been trained by her predecessor to do the report at 3:00 every afternoon. Data was collected at many different points and was all sent to this one person by 3:00 p.m. each day. She then manually summarized all of the day's booked sales by product class. She placed the completed report on top of the sales file cabinet by 4:30 p.m. The next morning, whoever used the report had picked it up and it was gone.

One evening, I was checking out some other data when I noticed a member of the cleaning crew pick up the daily sales report. "Excuse me," I asked. "What do you do with that report?"

"Well, we used to let them stack up on the cabinet, but then they got too heavy to carry easily, so we started to remove them every night." This was fascinating. "I put them in a box in the closet and each week we take the box out to the trash. I've been doing it that way for years."

Further research uncovered that the company owner had requested the report over eight years earlier. He had decided that it did not really serve his purposes, but he never thought to stop its production. For eight years, every new person was instructed on how to compile the report. For eight years, a person spent over an hour every day creating the report. And for eight years, no one had ever looked at the report other than to move it to the trash.

This was an easy one to fix. The report was eliminated. Just as in the earlier example, it would have been easy to fix the symptoms by speeding up the process or eliminating most of the manual effort. But the correct answer was to ask "why" and eliminate the actual problem.

Answer: It is so difficult to reconcile all the outbound freight bills and it slows down our ability to invoice our customers.

What was done? Here is another problem that is common to many businesses. They wait until the freight bill is received before sending an invoice to the customer so that the proper shipping charges can be added. The process is cumbersome, as every invoice for shipped product must be filed and then retrieved when the freight charges arrive. Then, the appropriate freight is added to each invoice so it can finally be sent to the customer.

This process caused numerous concerns. First, it increased the days outstanding for accounts receivable. Real money collection was being delayed with a very real cost that could be attached to each invoice affected. Second, it added a tremendous amount of extra work. No one ever thought to look at the cost versus the benefits.

Asking "why" in this case did not highlight an underlying problem. The process itself was the problem. Fixing it would require some different thinking.

For almost all shipments, the approximate shipping cost is easily calculated. There are charts, tables, and computer programs that can give you a very accurate answer based on the weight, size, and the from/to addresses. The calculated figures will normally be within pennies of the actual shipping amount. The first fear articulated was that an incorrect calculation would rob the company of profits. After a little research, we found that the number and amounts of errors made in the past were so small that even if every loss was allowed to stand, the savings in processing costs would more than make up for the added cost of unrecovered freight.

By rounding all freight costs up to the nearest whole dollar, a sufficient cushion would be created to cover any shortfall. Actually, it would generate a small profit—and the added cost was so little per account that very few customers ever noticed or complained (and those that did were given some compensation in return for allowing the company to use the simpler procedure).

In another company, they actually marked the freight up by a nominal percentage and made it a profit center. Why not? This was an opportunity that made sense.

CHAPTER 10

How to Ask the Questions

So how should you ask the two questions? The easiest thing is to just ask! You may want to explain what you are trying to accomplish. It always helps to present examples and encourage participation.

Many companies like to hold meetings to ask for input. Sometimes, asking a group of eight to ten people will reduce the intimidation factor. For smaller companies, forget the formal meeting. Invite a team (or the whole staff from one or more areas) to a simple lunch gathering to explain what you are looking for. Give everyone a notebook as explained earlier and watch the fun begin.

Larger companies will gravitate toward the meeting format. Enthusiasm and initial ideas become contagious and encourage thinking about what is being done in the business. All of a sudden, there are lots of new ideas. One-on-one meetings also work well in specific situations.

Step one is deciding who gets invited to the party. The first response from most managers is to invite the management team. This would be the wrong answer. The management team should be thinking about these issues all the time. Bringing them in is helpful only if they are not doing their jobs on a regular basis. Resist the urge.

The best information will come from the people closest to the action—the clerical people, the warehouse staff, and line people throughout the organization. Depending on the size of the company, it may take a number of small group meetings to get the full value.

If the meetings are too large, they will become intimidating and cause most line people to fear speaking up. However, if the meetings are too small there is no safety in numbers. The best groups are between eight and sixteen people. The attendees should also be from different areas and have different backgrounds. Diversity is an important element in assembling a group that will come up with the best answers.

Carefully select people who have positive attitudes. Especially when you are first starting, do not allow one person to ruin the process. Pick "go-to" people whom others seek out for answers. They usually have a great understanding of what happens (and often, why). See the next chapter on how to invite them.

When you are just beginning, there is often one more necessity: an outsider. Think about it—when was the last time anyone asked employees to find mistakes that their bosses have made? This is not an easy question for most people to answer. They will believe (rightly or wrongly) that they will only get in trouble for pointing out obvious problems. Remember, they have been taught from an early age that it is bad to be wrong.

A good facilitator (whether internal to the company or from the outside) will make them feel at ease. The right person will provide an atmosphere of trust and safety for sharing ideas. Without the boss in the room, most line people will be more willing to speak up.

The facilitator should at least be from outside the area or specific organization being examined. In general, facilitators should not participate in the meeting—they have too much power to hijack the process and destroy any results. This is a natural tendency, and another reason why it is so important to have someone from outside the group running the meeting. The facilitator should have an objective perspective on the issues being discussed; it is almost impossible to have a successful meeting if one of the participants (who always has his or her own agenda) is also managing the meeting process.

If chosen correctly, an experienced facilitator will help your people succeed. He or she will help them get good ideas on the table and develop them with integrity. Along the way, your staff will learn to facilitate meetings and will be able to assist in other areas of the company, where they can be independent.

Just get started on the right foot. The old saying is true, "You never get a second chance to make a first impression." Do everything possible to make sure the first experience is a good one. The rest of the process depends on it.

Later, it will be easier to include management personnel as everyone starts to experience the positive results from the process. When they see that no one is getting fired for speaking up; when they see ideas being implemented; and when they see rewards being handed out, then it will be easier to mix up teams and look for even more complex situations to tackle.

Consider making a list of three to five people you can take to lunch to try out the questions. Once you identify them, go to the next chapter and create an invitation.

CHAPTER 11

Inviting the Meeting Participants

When selecting participants for the first meetings, start with the superstar workers. These are the individuals who will be most willing to put ideas on the table for discussion. They have more self-confidence and will see the selection as an opportunity to make an impact on the operation. Consider inviting a representative from each of the major areas of the company. For example, one person can represent all of accounting—or, if appropriate, you can select one person from accounts receivable, accounts payable, and financial reporting.

Invite the selected individuals to a short pre-meeting. Tell them about what is going to be done. Give them some ideas of things to look for and introduce the two questions.

As noted earlier, one easy way to help encourage participation is to provide everyone with a small spiral notebook or flip book to carry with them at all times. During the next week (or month), they should be asked to keep jotting notes every time they see something dumb or difficult (opportunities in disguise). This will make the collection easier, and it creates a bit of competition as everyone starts to compare how many pages of notes they have taken.

In addition, after the process gets rolling, they should be asked to go back to their departments and explain to their peers what is being done. They should tell the rest of the team that they will be representing the department in a very important first step toward improving operations. These individuals should let the other employees know that everyone is being asked to participate by uncovering dumb and difficult things that can be brought up at a meeting to be held in the very near future.

Someone from upper management or HR can be provided if the selected worker would like help with these department meetings. Just make sure the individual executive that you choose is respected by the operation he or she is going to visit. Be careful of any hidden agendas or old baggage. You want the greatest potential for success.

For smaller companies, the first group can be more focused (select an area to concentrate on) or can cover the total operation. Take the three to five selected employees out to lunch. Explain what you want to accomplish. Give each one his or her small spiral notebook. Consider asking them to find one quick thing to write down before they leave the lunch. It will help them get started. Then tell them you want to get back together in a week. It is that easy.

When inviting individuals, you will need to develop a standard invitation. It needs to explain what is being done and why. While this may sound self-serving, giving all participants a copy of this book will make it easier for them to understand what is being asked of them and the kinds of ideas they might find. The many examples will help jog their thinking and produce better results in a shorter period of time.

The actual invitation should make recipients feel like they have been selected as part of a very exclusive group. Let them know the company is looking to them to pioneer a new program of continuous improvement. Tell them this is the beginning of something special that will transform the company and prepare it for a sustainable, successful future.

Give them at least one week to prepare; two weeks may be better if they seem nervous about the idea. In that case, meet with the participants individually after a couple of days. See how they are doing. Encourage them. Ask to see what they are gathering in their books.

Be prepared to help with any questions and to clear roadblocks. Historically, most early questions have to do with boundaries, so the local politics will need to be set aside to get the most value possible.

One more note on timing: Three weeks is too long a time from the introduction to the first real meeting. People will lose focus. They will forget what they are supposed to do. Enthusiasm will wane.

For larger groups, holding at least one more pre-meeting can be useful after a week of note collecting. It will prove it is safe to come up with examples, provide some laughs, and, more important, it will help the group become more comfortable with one another in advance of the big meeting. This session should take place only four or five business days after the kickoff. Doing it quickly will give procrastinators a nominal kick in the backside and get them started.

After the first group has met and ideas are being implemented and publicized, the word will spread. You may be surprised at the number of people who want to participate. As a matter of fact, one of the issues many companies run into is how to limit the number of sessions—at least in the beginning.

Once you get going, informal groups are more than welcome.

Get as many people as possible involved. Everyone has a different viewpoint that will lead to diverse contributions.

Once you have a few successes, the team will be on a roll. Give them freedom to shoot any sacred cows. Help them to take more control.

CHAPTER 12

Identifying Constraints

Constraints are one of the limiting factors many companies impose. Try to eliminate as many constraints as possible. In sessions I run, we purposely tell the participants not to consider time, cost, or available technology. We will have plenty of time later on to bring reality into the conversation. Most people do not know what is possible, so it is better to let them dream and come up with the industry-changing ideas first. Then do the research to figure out how those ideas can be implemented.

For example, I was given a problem related to sorting mail for a Fortune 500 company. It may seem insignificant, but getting the mail for six thousand people spread across three campuses to the right person quickly and accurately was critical for the successful operation of the organization (and this was before e-mail, when everyone relied on getting data on paper).

The two greatest problems we had to resolve were related to the training time for a new sorter (two to three months under the old system) and errors made in the effort to memorize the names of the people who received the most mail.

The solution we dreamed up was to use voice recognition. Under this new system, the operator would read the first initial of the first name and the first four letters of the last name of the mail recipient into a microphone. The system would then display any matches. Tim Johnson and Taylor Johnston would have the same code, so duplicates would be shown with the full name and a title. This would allow the operator to resolve over 99 percent of all situations with matching codes. Then the system would show the campus (there were three in the city), building, floor, wing, and mail stop. All information would be written on the envelope and placed in a "first sort" mailbag without putting down the pencil or any other intervening action.

It is always fun to ask audiences when they think the application described here was put in place. Most people will guess sometime in the last five years. Every once in a while I will get a joker who says, "Twenty years ago." They are getting closer. The actual start-up happened in 1973. Voice recognition has been around for a long time. But, outside of a few technical people, it was not widely recognized as a usable and relatively inexpensive technology. That is why it is important not to let concerns about the availability of technology get in the way of dreaming about potential solutions. There are some amazing capabilities out there if we just look for them.

The next constraint that needs to be eliminated is cost. If everyone focuses on the cost of a new idea, it will die a quick death. Hold off on the cost until the solutions are well thought out. At the end of the process, the cost may be immaterial compared to the savings. If the idea is rejected too soon, you will never have the opportunity to learn what the real return might be.

In any organization, there will be ideas that do not work. In one project at a large financial services firm, we defined a process we called "accelerated failure." History had taught us that not every idea was good. If an analysis showed it had promise, their management team was always willing to take a chance—as long as the ideas were tested in limited situations where their applicability and potential success could be easily and rapidly demonstrated. By the same token, an idea that did not accomplish its goal was scrapped before it was widely implemented.

Even more important, the management team never came back and blamed the people who generated the idea. On the contrary, they were recognized for trying. Then the idea was put back into the mix to see if it could be improved and tested again. Not only was failure unpunished, it was celebrated, though not to the exclusion of celebrating success. Successful ideas had bigger celebrations, simply to prove they were a natural part of running an innovative business.

Management has a responsibility to all stakeholders to make sure that even good ideas are not implemented when the cost benefit ratio falls below a predetermined threshold. Just do not eliminate good ideas before they can be massaged and improved.

There is one other constraint worth mentioning—members of the team often known as roadblocks. Know who they are. Plan to keep them in the loop, but under close scrutiny. Make it clear that interference will not be allowed. Then work with them over time to show how they can make a positive contribution to moving the company forward.

CHAPTER 13

Knocking Out Killer Phrases

In companies where negativity has been a problem in the past, we introduce an exercise to identify "killer phrases" that cannot be used during the project or by management at the review. These phrases are listed on flip charts and then distributed to everyone during the research phase. The most common killer phrases are

- We have *never* done it *that* way.
- We have *always* done it *this* way.
- It is not in the budget.
- John (or Mary) will not allow it.
- It will never work here.
- IT will block it.
- We tried that before.
- If it ain't broke, don't fix it.

The last two are the most dangerous. Something that did not work back in the Stone Age has no relevance today. Talk to the youngest workers and you will start to understand that the Stone Age just ended a couple of years ago. Fantastic advances in technology mean that something that could not work six months ago may be easy today. The speed of technological growth is amazing.

The "if it ain't broke" phrase creates more emergencies than almost anything else. Think about it. When does anything break? When it is under pressure. This killer phrase suggests that you wait until your system or equipment are under the greatest pressure and then watch them fail when there is no time left to fix them. Then you have to do quick-and-dirty fixes because you cannot take time to do it right. For any organization, it is best to fix failures before they occur. Predict what can go wrong (or learn from what has happened in the past) and fix things when there is limited time pressure, or none at all.

In many situations, we establish a penalty if someone is caught using a killer phrase. You could try collecting a dollar in a pot every time one is used, to be donated at the end of the quarter. This makes it fun to catch others who would otherwise be a negative influence while raising some money for a favorite charity.

Do not limit the areas that can be examined. Keep it open and free in order to find the best opportunities. Over time, no area of the business should be left untouched. You do not know what can be improved unless you ask. Remember, Mark Twain said sacred cows make the best hamburger.

Experience tells us that the group will not have trouble coming up with answers. The most difficult thing when beginning this process is convincing the staff that it is safe to tell the boss that something they have been told to do is dumb!

Some groups may need encouragement and constant help to keep going. For example, in one situation, a group came up with a great idea to reduce the effort required to complete a process. The team worked hard and as a result eliminated the need for one full-time employee. Instead of celebrating the success and moving that person into a role of helping other groups, management let one of the team members go.

What a horrible signal. Help the company and get fired. That was the end of continuous improvement in that company. It took years before anyone was willing to be part of a team to save the company any required effort again. Instead, the opposite began to happen. People learned to make the systems less efficient so they could guarantee the safety of their jobs.

Before starting down this road, top management and the ownership group *must* commit to not firing any employee as a result of improved operations. Each potentially displaced worker needs to be retrained and moved to another position of equal or higher pay and responsibility. Companies should take advantage of using their best employees and the extra time to get out of do-do and get the important things done. Focus on real opportunities and send a positive message to everyone in your organization.

When groups find it difficult to identify any waste, any dumb processes, or anything that is considered difficult, it is usually a sign of mistrust or another systemic issue that is keeping people from being comfortable with participating.

No organizations exist that do not have room for improvement. A lack of staff input is a very loud and clear signal to management. Some of the issues to look into include a lack of support from the middle management team, a history of not listening, or even negative consequences for staff who tried to participate in earlier programs.

In this type of situation, take a step back. Have the most trusted person in the management group open a dialog with one or two of the "go-to" people on staff. See if they can be enlisted to help spread the word that no one will be hurt by helping. Any manager who is against the process should be kept away from the group meetings.

It is not always easy to repair years of "abuse" (that may be a little harsh, but it does present the problem in stark terms). If there is a long history of distrust in the company, it may take a well-orchestrated meeting with publicized results to show what can be accomplished.

People will probably want to see if there are any long-term negative consequences for the participants. So, wait a couple of months before starting the next small group. Build upon successes. It may be slow going at first, but the end results will be worth the wait if the company is truly committed to making this process work.

In some tough cases, an organization may want to consider practicing on a small group of middle managers. This will give the team some valuable experience before working with the general line staff. Managers should be more willing to accept the experimentation and the risk that goes along with it. (If they are not, the operation has problems to correct that exceed the scope of this book.) This approach will also provide an example that everyone else can watch in action.

Observe the process closely. Understand how different members of the team react. If something goes wrong, get input and fix the process prior to using it with the staff. For example, if you have planned to wait one week between the kickoff and the actual meeting but find it has caused too much stress due to the heavy workload, then be willing to provide extra time. The participants should not feel as if they are on a death march, but instead that they are part of a team helping to improve their company.

When you are ready to get started, there are just a couple of reminders. Following up on an earlier comment, make sure someone from outside the group is the facilitator—the person running the meeting. That person should not have a stake in the meeting so they cannot be accused of trying to take sides. The right person will be a positive addition to the process and should be asked to start by letting members of the group list their own killer phrases.

Second, when possible have the meetings offsite, or at least away from the telephones and general interruptions of the day. Make sure that staff knows this is paid time and that you value their input. Please see the material in the "Extras" section (beginning on page 131) on holding meetings. It includes ideas on location, setup, and timing.

Give yourself at least one half day to get the ideas flowing. Breakfast and/or lunch are a big deal to most line personnel. Make them feel like big shots and you will benefit immeasurably.

Many first-level supervisors and middle managers spend a lot of their operational time in meetings, so it is no wonder that over the years, many employees comment specifically about the meeting process. Plan the meetings carefully and take advantage of the willingness of your employees to participate.

CHAPTER 14

Managing the Meeting

So, what happens in one of these meetings? There are many possibilities. Often, there will be one person who says, "Every day I have to do X for the Y group. It just does not make sense. It seems like a waste of time."

One of your employees is sticking his or her neck out and everyone is watching to see how you will react. Be positive. Do not even think about reacting negatively—no matter what is brought up. Whatever is said first, find something you can celebrate about it and build on that. In this case, ask people from Group Y (if they are not already in the room, get them there—or call them up at the last minute and put them on conference call) to respond and give their input. Ask them to walk the other group through the process and explain what they do with X.

There are two common conversations paths that usually result. First, Group Y might say, "We've never understood why you keep sending us X. It has always seemed like a waste of time and we do not use it. We just figured someone else needed it and we were stuck on some copy list."

In this case, have a good laugh and then check carefully that no one else is using the output of the process. As soon as you can validate that it is not being used, stop doing it. The staff will love you. They will save time that can be used for other important things that need to get done. They will see a positive result from the questioning process and will be encouraged to work harder to find more areas to improve.

The second conversation path is that Group Y will explain how important the information is to them, how it is used, and why. Then the original group that brought up the problem may say, "Wow, we never realized what it was used for. If we can just change Z, we can accomplish the same result with much less effort." Then examine the process again and make sure there are no other users who should be contacted before implementing the change.

Keep the atmosphere positive and you will keep the team generating new ideas. Better yet, positive stories about the process will spread through the company and more people will want to participate and share ideas. When this happens, you have reached the pinnacle. Your organization is becoming one of continuous improvement. That will serve you well for a long time to come.

You can help the word spread by publicizing the results. Use an internal newsletter or intranet site to brag about what occurred. Consider a public celebration of the individuals who came up with the questions and solutions. These actions will help make sure the whole company knows about the process and feels encouraged to participate in the future.

If you treat the questions as a quick fix or the flavor of the month and do not follow up, you will have wasted your time and lost an excellent opportunity to bring your staff into the improvement strategy of the company. There is long-term value in allowing your people to feel part of the solution. Give them a stake in the future of the company and you will be amazed at what they can accomplish.

Most management teams are surprised when we first open the

gates to ideas from their staff. Once the process gets rolling, however, there are so many opportunities for small and large gains. The positive results add up quickly.

CHAPTER 15

Implementing Change

Once you ask people to help and prove you are serious, ideas will start to flow in. Most employees are thrilled to be consulted. As a matter of fact, many of them have provided ideas in the past and were put down for even thinking they might have an idea that their manager could not see.

When you propose the questions to them, let everyone know this is a new day. The old NIH (not invented here) put-down will not be used. Let them know you are really interested in what they have to say and that you want to take advantage of what they see every day that management misses.

You need to refine raw ideas and define metrics (discussed in chapter 6) so that a starting point can be established. A formal evaluation of the cost and expected return on investment must be completed before you can give the "go ahead."

You should assemble a team to work on the ideas. Again, diversity in the team will be important. If you only have personnel from the accounting area, too much emphasis will be placed on financial aspects. The same is true if the majority of team members are from the sales force or from any specific department. It is the team's job to research and massage the ideas to create something that can have outsized returns based on the required investment of resources, and they need to think about multiple areas of the company to do this.

Once ideas are ready to be presented to top management, keep the team informed as to what is happening. Consider inviting the idea team to be part of the presentation. (In this case, a preliminary meeting should be held with the executive team to prepare them to have a positive meeting with staff.) It is very important that this meeting is seen as an open-minded review of the idea and a celebration of the process.

When you begin to get input, you may feel overwhelmed with the number of ideas generated. That is a wonderful problem to have. Take advantage of the good ideas by setting up a simple method to collect, document, and organize them.

Simple is always key. If the process is complex or difficult, it will not be done. There are many tools available, from spreadsheets to basic database managers, that will allow you to set up and maintain an idea repository.

Next, select a *small* committee (no more than five people) made up of top executives who will be responsible for prioritizing the opportunities (and taking the flak or blame from people and groups whose ideas were given a lower priority). Of course, there will be lobbying from the troops, but that is a good thing. Make sure the committee considers all input, potential returns, resource requirements, and timing.

One medium-sized company we worked with was having trouble setting their priorities. There was a backlog of requests for IT support (which was a red flag that there were other problems). In this case, the IT manager reacted to squeaky wheels and tried to do so many projects at once that none got done.

The manager did not like conflict and tried to please too many bosses. By simply making prioritization the responsibility of top management (he was still part of the committee), the work was finally organized and prioritized, and individual projects were managed from start to finish.

Once put under a top-management microscope, many of the "quick hit" requests that were "critical to my area" were dropped. They could not be justified. They were not well thought out. And since there was no incentive to conserve limited resources, everyone just asked for everything they thought might help.

One larger company put in a chargeback system. Each department asking for a project was charged for the effort. Two great things happened as a result. First, the number of requests declined immediately. The department heads started to review all requests to make sure they were reasonable, would help the operation, and had a payback of less than a year.

Second, the IT department became much more "customer" oriented. This was because top management made one other important change. The chargebacks were the funding for the department. If others were not satisfied with the work done, they could refuse to make the payment. Very quickly, IT understood their future depended on happy customers, and their attitude adjustment was quickly visible to the whole organization.

IT is an easy example to understand. It is the same elsewhere in the organization. The committee should look for the very quick hits first. What can you do without a large investment of resources? Can you simply eliminate a step in an out-of-date process? Can you easily change a procedure without any programming effort? These are the first ideas to implement. Taking action on these opportunities will set the stage and prove there is value in all the ideas that are being suggested. It will show the staff you are serious. It will create enthusiasm, and there are few things as contagious as enthusiasm.

To help ignite the enthusiasm, one company even started an award system. Each month one person was selected to get the trophy (it could be a plaque, a real trophy, or even an unusual paperweight). This company included a small monetary reward as well. Each month the previous six winners would meet to select the next winner (and none of them could repeat while on the "winners committee"). Then the trophy would be awarded at a lunch gathering of the staff.

This was fun. The staff looked forward to it. The public display of gratitude from management was appreciated. And each month more people submitted ideas. The enthusiasm really was contagious.

As the low-hanging fruit is used up, start to look for return on investment. What will give you an outsized return for any investment of time or effort? All the while, keep looking for new ideas. When a new quick hit is brought to your attention, implement it ASAP. Do not make it wait.

For a larger opportunity or one that will require a significant investment, it is not always easy to do the return-on-invest calculation. This is especially true when the enhancement will improve a hard-to-measure value like "customer satisfaction."

This is where members of management earn their pay. Tough decisions will have to be made. Think through how you would measure the positive results of each opportunity and attempt to assign a value. Your system may not always be 100 percent accurate, but it should help you focus on the high-value items first.

One example was a client who decided to help their customers become more profitable. The question was really a statement: "Our customers are so dumb that they do not understand how much more money they could make." It led to an industry-changing question: "Why don't we help our customers run a better business?"

Since this would be something no one else had done, and no

one in the company had ever done, the fear of failure was high. The process took a lot of thought, interviews, research, and some real soul searching.

While there was no specific number that management could point to, they made some assumptions (that proved overly conservative in the long run) to build a case for the new project. The idea was to write a computer program specifically tailored to improve their customers' abilities to make a better profit.

After much gnashing of teeth, the company undertook the project. It was almost the largest investment bet the company had ever made. Still, if it worked, they assumed their average amount of business from an average customer would go from just under 40 percent to over 75 percent. If the program were picked up by as little as 10 percent of the customer base, the new sales would pay for the development.

The good news was that after a few years, they had penetrated over 70 percent of their own customer base. The sales percentage did not stop at 75 percent, but came close to 95 percent. On top of that, the number of new customers attracted to the company jumped by hundreds of percent for the next couple of years. It all started with a simple question and management's willingness to consider something "way out there."

When looking at new processes, improvements in efficiency can exceed 30 percent in many organizations. The older the organization, the more entrenched the operations, and the older the existing automation, the more opportunities we usually find.

Think about the savings when the "closet report" described in chapter 9 (the one that was thrown out every night without ever being looked at) was ended. Suddenly one overworked clerk had an extra ninety minutes each day to apply to important tasks. That is real value!

No matter how you implement the change, come back and revisit the process a week or two after the solution is implemented to see how it's working. If you are lucky, you will find that the groups are talking to each other between meetings and have fine-tuned the process to make it even better without you directing them.

You may also find that by discussing the process, your team will discover other things that can be modified to improve the workflow. As you build trust in this process, give your teams the authority to implement simple changes that will smooth out processing. You will save time and gain the benefits much quicker.

Sure, there will be mistakes, but accept them as part of the team's education. Each experience will make them better decision makers. Help them learn to continuously improve what they are doing. Show them how to use feedback to refine ideas and get greater benefits. Give them a little leeway and you will be rewarded over and over.

There will be some procedures that cannot be changed. Research might identify reasons to keep them the old way. When that happens, call the team together (with all of the appropriate groups represented) and talk through the findings.

If you have to maintain an old operational process, it is okay. Do it with a smile and make sure everyone sees it as a positive step of learning. People should be thanked for highlighting a possible dumb thing or for revealing that the new way would not work.

After the first round of improvements, the ideas do not dry up. They do become more complex. Once the low-hanging fruit is picked, there will still be plenty of ideas to go after; they may just require a bit more reach.

The second set of ideas may take longer to implement, and the savings will take a bit longer to realize. Just do not give up. Establishing a culture of improvement will serve your company well into the future.

The same two questions continue to work. We just need to find more people to ask. New employees and temporary workers are a wonderful source of fresh ideas. They are not as invested in how you do things.

They bring different experiences and perspectives to the table, and for a couple of weeks, they will easily be able to spot dumb and hard things. After that time, they may become part of the problem. They learn how you do things and can no longer see the problems as clearly.

An easy way to keep your employees finding opportunities is to make it into a contest. Have a good time and keep the environment fun, safe, and encouraging. It is not difficult and the rewards will make it more than worthwhile, for both you and your staff.

CHAPTER 16

Additional Examples

Answer: We spend too much time trying to save every new employee, even if they have a very small potential to make it.

What was done? A growing organization needed to hire field salespeople to fill new offices that were being opened at a rapid pace. It took over a year to train and prepare new people to sell on their own. An additional two or three years was required for those salespeople to become self-sustaining and profitable. The problem was that there were many failures, and the recruiters just considered that to be a cost of doing business. Then one of the sales coaches asked, "Why do we keep trying to save the under-performers instead of concentrating on the stars?" What a great dumb question.

The first answer was, "We want everyone to succeed. It is only right that we help anyone we hired to do well. It is our responsibility; we hired them." This answer begged a second question, "Do we ever make a mistake?" It was not necessary to wait for an answer.

The first step was to calculate the cost of failure. No one had ever looked at this. By doing a bit of historical research, the cost was calculated. The surprise was how the cost escalated as the time in training and in a field office increased. The historical records also showed that only a small handful of the slow performers who received all of the extra attention had ever succeeded in the firm. It was determined that postponing the inevitable was costly and harmful to everyone involved.

At the end of the process, it was decided that "accelerated failure" was the best avenue for the company. Again, using historical records, a sales curve was plotted that traced the average increases in accepted metrics (revenue, new customers, number of sales calls made, etc.) by month for successful sales reps. New people who did not stay within a nominal percentage of the curve were let go after one warning. It may have seemed harsh, but it helped everyone. The new hire that was not going to make it moved on to a (hopefully) better job for them. The company focused their efforts on the best reps and reduced the time it took them to become self-supporting, reduced the number of failures late in the game, cut the cost of training, and increased the profitability of the whole firm.

Answer: It does not make sense that we are paying fuel costs when our outside people purchase gas-guzzlers that cannot be justified by their job or their responsibilities.

What was done? A company with an extensive outside sales force was watching reimbursements for fuel escalate with the run up in oil costs in the early 2000s. The cost of supporting the staff fuel expenses was becoming a significant drag on profits; it was not difficult to see how an extra dollar a gallon could really hurt.

Every salesperson turned in gas receipts with their "call reports" and was paid for whatever gas they used. The sales force favored large SUVs. Then one of the clerks working on expense reports suggested in an offhand comment, "Why don't we replace all of these SUVs with hybrids?" Another questioner finds a dumb thing that can be fixed.

The CFO was very approachable and the clerk, along with her supervisor, asked the question again. The reaction was one of great interest. The CFO immediately started doing a number of calculations. A leasing specialist was called in to provide some cost analysis and ultimately a formal proposal.

Not counting the value they might get from being able to advertise themselves as going "green," they found that the savings in gas (going from an average of 14 mpg to about 40 mpg) could just about pay for the new cars.

Even though the model they wanted was in demand, an order for fifty vehicles carries weight in any market. Of course, there was grumbling. The salespeople had been able to ignore the increase in gas prices because the company just kept paying for whatever they used.

Now they were being given much smaller cars to drive and were required to keep track of nonbusiness mileage (for tax purposes). As a side benefit, the company gained much more accurate reporting.

In short order, the salespeople found that the cars attracted attention and helped them sell the fact that they were interested in the customer's ability to save wherever possible. The grumbling died down and people even enjoyed the new hybrid cars.

Answer: We keep "will call" products on the pick-up shelf for weeks when it is obvious no one is coming to pick them up.

What was done? "Will call" is a process in many distribution and wholesale businesses that allows customers to call and request an item before they leave their location. It is supposed to be an easy way to make sure that what customers need is in stock and to eliminate waiting time when they arrive to pick the items up.

The order is pulled from inventory and the sales slip is written up. Then it is put on the "will call" shelf so that when buyers come in, it is very easy to give them the order, get the shipping ticket signed, and send them on their way back to the plant or job site as quickly as possible.

The problem is, many of those orders are never picked up. The reasons vary. Most of the time (based on an unscientific sample) the buyer found the same product at a lower price or a closer location. The first wholesaler called was used to guarantee availability and to get a starting price. The buyer could then use these facts to negotiate for better pricing, but with the knowledge there was a backup that could always be picked up.

Most of the early suggestions to fix the situation ran into tears from the sales force. According to some members of the sales team, charging customers who did not pick up their will call items would lead to "a mass exodus of some of our best customers." Of course, a quick investigation proved that this was incorrect. Most of the "never-picked-up items" were from the least profitable customers who only seemed to buy from the company as a last resort.

The solution included a couple of new actions. The first, and the easiest, was to institute an immediate charge on a credit card for each product ordered. Customers were told their card was being charged and when the product would be ready. Right away, many callers changed their minds and said they would call back. Those who allowed their cards to be charged almost always came by to pick up the merchandise. The number of items left on the shelf dropped to almost zero.

The second new procedure was to make it a published policy to charge a "restocking" fee of 20 percent or $5.00, whichever was more, to put an item back on the shelf and reverse the charge. The problem of abandoned will call items went away. In a very few cases, "A" customers were given a pass if they only had one or two unpicked-up will calls in a year. There was no loss of customers, just good riddance to a lot of wasted time.

Answer: We are afraid to admit that some of our biggest customers are not profitable.

What was done? In too many companies, we make the assumption that the customer with the largest volume is the one we need to protect the most. This is not necessarily true, but often no one is willing to challenge the status quo.

Most companies do not measure (or know how to measure) the value of a customer; therefore, they cannot know which ones are the best or the worst. In this instance, we started by obtaining agreement on a simple statement: "A good customer is one we make a profit on."

Next, we had to decide how to measure profitability. This proved to be more difficult than it should have been. In the end, we decided to calculate a customer's contribution to gross profit. The company's sales force agreed to take the total sales dollars and subtract all discounts; charges for all outstanding receivables over fifteen days (using current interest rates); the cost for each order (a charge for opening an order and then for each line item after the first); uncollected delivery charges; salespeople's commissions; and the cost for special services (including training, returns, engineering support, etc.).

The first reports that were produced caused a great deal of terror. The sales force was sure the numbers were wrong because they showed that some of the accounts that were always celebrated due to their size were actually unprofitable.

The company launched a new program to increase profitability on all accounts. The idea was to start charging for special services first. This would be easy to monitor and if any customer did not like it, they could always obtain those services elsewhere.

The sales force felt they were stuck in the middle. The easy life was officially over. Those who had rested on their laurels were suddenly forced to get out and really sell. They had to get their customers behind the change or risk losing a great deal of income. It was not easy, but the changes were made.

Very quickly, some customers were "fired." If the customer thought they deserved free services, even as an unprofitable account, they were encouraged to "find someone else to put out of business." In many cases, the customer backed down and accepted the new charges. (We think they tried to shop for the same deal elsewhere and could not get it.)

When customers did leave, about 30 percent eventually came back. The rest were better off buying elsewhere, for everyone concerned—except the new distributor, who was now losing money on that customer even if they did not know it.

It was not easy to make the new changes stick. It took a great deal of discipline on the part of sales management. Over time, the new rules had the desired effect. Customer profitability increased and ranking became important. True "A" customers got special services, but they were earned rather than given away.

Before leaving this topic, many of the companies we consult have taken the process one step further. They use the same type of criteria to measure all of their suppliers and business partners (banks, insurance agents, etc.). It is amazing what you can learn by putting metrics against any group to understand who is best and worst for your operation. The next story is a great example.

Answer: Now that we have created all of these great metrics, we keep them secret. For some reason, we treat the salespeople's results as if they were confidential payroll reports, and in a way, they are.

What was done? This issue was a conflict between a seemingly "dumb" thing and a requirement for privacy about what a person was earning. Upon reflection, it became easy to understand that it was reasonable to publish contribution to gross margin prior to paying sales commissions. It was also appropriate to implement a number of other measures that could aid in managing a sales force, such as monitoring the number of new customers and the increases in sales and margin contribution from existing customers.

Once the management team was able to gain insight into all of the comparisons, a number of clear patterns emerged. These were critical in controlling what was being sold and for what amounts.

Further, it was decided that competition within the organization would be healthy. This meant that the "pick, pack, ship" teams would be compared on the number of errors tracked back to their group and all results would be displayed publicly. But ultimately, publishing the sales results was what caused the greatest upheaval.

Using the concept originated by Mike Marks at Indian River Consulting, each week the company would list the Champs of the Camp and the Chumps of the Dump. Salespeople at the bottom were on notice to get better or get out. It was not really that harsh, but the message was clear. You would not survive long if you were always at the bottom of the list.

It did take a while to make sure everyone was being measured in a fair way. Adjustments were made for time on the job, product lines, government regulation, and so on. Still, it became pretty obvious who was working and who was coasting.

The turnaround in attitude was quick. The changes in strategy, sharing of information, and results showed up quickly on the top and bottom lines. The friendly competition worked, and another dumb thing proved to be worth its weight in gold.

Answer: Often, when we send out a page to field service or salespeople, when they finally call in no one knows who sent the page or for what reason.

What was done? For younger employees reading this case, there was a time, not too long ago, when sophisticated companies gave their field people pagers. When you wanted someone, you would send a signal that would cause a device on that person's belt to ring or buzz. Then the person could look at a short display of up to ten numbers. Mostly it displayed the phone number to call for information. Other people used the display for sending messages. For example, a 911 meant there was an emergency and to call immediately. A 411 signaled an information request and to call back when convenient. It was a very advanced way to get great value from a simple device. (Please note this example happened in ancient history—back in the early days of voice mail. Even though it may seem quaint today, ask yourself if you would have taken a chance and suggested the following solution. Then ask yourself what is happening today that could give you the same opportunity for improving operations.)

At this company, the owner thought the pager question was a good one. He had been considering adding a new voice mail system, and thought this question could be the justification he was looking for. Instead of having to look for the right person, each field person would be assigned a voice mailbox. Now, when people needed to communicate, they could just leave a voice mail with all of the details. Then they would send out a standard page. Upon receipt, the field people would call their assigned voice mailboxes when they were able and retrieve the messages.

This system eliminated all of the wasted time associated with the original process. It improved communications. It improved customer service. All in all, the rewards completely justified the voice mail system.

Even better, the company started to brainstorm how to get additional value from voice mail. Back in those days, we still had secretaries who transcribed dictation tapes. To speed up the process, all salespeople were given a voice mailbox for their assigned secretary. After a sales call, they could call in all of their notes and dictate thank-you messages and other memos from the road.

Field salespeople became much more efficient. Their evenings at hotels would start with a phone call to the voice mail. By the time they returned to the office, letters, memos, and other instructions were waiting for signature. It saved at least one day and spread out the secretarial work.

A separate company even started to use voice mail for field service people to call in their time and parts used on each service call. This reduced errors and allowed invoices to be prepared while the service people were on the way to another call (instead of hoping they would turn in all of the paperwork the next time they came into the office), and it was readable.

Some of these ideas may seem quaint, but they were breakthroughs when implemented. Use this process as an opportunity to find dumb or hard things that can be fixed by using some new or even existing capability in your company.

Answer: We cannot complete the printing of reports in our normal two shifts.

What was done? This example happened many years ago, but the lessons are still meaningful. The company requested options for developing their hardware to keep up with ever-expanding needs. The easy response was to cure the symptom; the right thing to do was to find the underlying problem.

The company was already running two full shifts to complete printing, collating, and distribution of all the computer reports—especially at month end. The easy answer was to purchase additional hardware and add capacity to produce more printing. One alternative they were ready to consider was to purchase an additional high-speed printer (this was before the broad availability of laser printers), and they needed to compare this to the possibility of adding a third shift for one week a month.

As the team analyzed the situation, it quickly became clear that they were printing enough reports to keep every employee in the company reading all month long without doing any "real" work. The correct first question had to be, "Do we really need all of these reports?"

With the permission of company leadership, at the end of the month only the most critical general ledger, payroll, and government-required reports were printed. Then, when people called to ask where their reports were, we told them the computer was down and it might be a week before we caught up.

If report recipients did not ask a second time, their report (or copy of a report) was discontinued. If they did call a second time, they were invited to a meeting where they were asked to justify why they got the report and explain exactly what they did with it. A large number answered that they just received the report and rarely used it. It was simply "part of the process" and they carefully filed them every period and then threw out the collected stack at the end of the year.

Others used the reports infrequently or were just nosey and wanted to know what was going on. Some copies were used to check on what others were doing, although they rarely found anything wrong that had to be corrected. In each case, the report copies were eliminated.

Of the remaining reports, the users were able to consolidate many separate printed reports into a smaller number by combining information and revising the output formats. By the time the process was completed, over half of all reports were eliminated. Instead of any new hardware or employees, the printing operation was reduced to a single shift, the amount of paper was drastically reduced, and dozens of file cabinets were eliminated.

Even though many reports are produced online today, we still need to be careful about what is being distributed. If people get reports, they may feel a need to review them. Unless there is a specific purpose, this is a waste of time. Too much information or the same information in too many formats can create confusion instead of clarity. Take the time during any process review to eliminate what you do not need.

Answer: We allow customers to take discounts they have not earned. Then, we have to do a tremendous amount of extra work to issue credit and debit memos, update records, and balance the accounts.

What was done? The common response from management when asked why they allow this to happen is always, "Everyone else does it. It is part of the competitive landscape. If we enforce the limits on discounts, we will lose our best customers. Any time someone pays extra, we just consider it a gift."

This is the wrong way to look at the situation. Most companies offer a discount of 1 or 2 percent for a payment received within ten to thirty days. Yet many customers take the discount and do not pay for forty-five to ninety days. Sometimes, to make themselves feel good, they actually write the check on the correct date (or at least date it that way) and do not mail it for a week or longer.

Abe WalkingBear Sanchez, one of the leading authorities on dealing with credit issues, sees this all the time. His suggestion is easy. Instead of allowing the customer to control the transaction, take control back. Change the rules. Indicate that payments received within the specified time frame will earn a credit that will be deducted from the next invoice.

That insures more business and on-time payments.

What do you do with the "A" customer who balks? My suggestion is that you tell them the 2 percent (or whatever number you want to use) has already been deducted. That saves everyone the extra effort and you will still be paid in the same number of days.

Answer: We are always breaking case quantities. We receive widgets (pick any product) in boxes of twelve each. There are a few customers who always want ten. The cost to open, count, repack, and then lose the remaining two has begun to exceed whatever we make on the sale.

What was done? In this situation, here is a good rule to follow: the cost of breaking a pack exceeds any profit on what you sold at the regular price unless you increase the cost. What does it cost to have a warehouse person open up the standard pack, count out the number of items requested, pack them in a new box/bag/package, add a barcode (so it can be priced and inventory updated), and then repack the remaining items?

Unless you increase the cost for buying less than a standard pack, you are almost guaranteed to lose money. If you feel you cannot raise the price (which is normally a wrong assumption), talk to the customer. Explain that the product is packed by the dozen. Then offer to sell them the dozen at the ten price. It will save you money.

A better solution, however, is to charge extra for breaking packs. That way, the cost for each item in quantities of ten (or five or six) is greater than the cost for twelve. It will convince many customers to switch.

If this is a major issue with many customers, call the supplier and see if they would be willing to change the pack size to ten. They may be willing and able to make the change for a small incremental cost. If the supplier will not do it, you may be able to get a sheltered workshop or idle employees to do it upon receipt of the product. By setting it up as a production process, it will cost less, take less time, be less disruptive, reduce the lost stock, and potentially add an extra pack to sell for every five orders (using the two leftovers that are normally lost).

Answer: We keep providing emergency services to customers who only call us in emergency situations—and expect our best pricing on top of it.

What was done? Sales thought the emergency service was a competitive necessity. If the company stopped offering it, customers would go elsewhere. However, as we looked into the situation, we did find that a number of special requests came from companies that were not regular or "A" customers. In these cases, the salespeople believed that this offer represented an opportunity to get their business.

The reality was that the non-customers who only used the company in an emergency were never going to change their primary purchasing behavior. All the company was doing was saving their normal supplier from servicing them.

In the case of the average customers, they assigned zero value to the service because that is what the company told them it was worth. An emergency service that is not invoiced has no intrinsic value. If the cost is zero, the value is zero. Even the best customers did not appreciate the cost of the emergency response, especially outside of normal business hours.

First, the company had to accurately determine the cost of these emergency services. If the company could not put a value on it, how could they expect customers to? By studying the number of emergency calls and the cost to open the warehouse or to send a special delivery truck for each incident, the company discovered new options. If opening the warehouse in the middle of the night to keep a plant operating costs you $300, then it is reasonable to cover your costs and make a profit by charging $450 for the service.

Next it became important to know who the company's best customers were. They needed to be able to segment customers into groups that would allow them to offer different service levels at different costs to different customers.

As a result, the following changes were implemented. First, any time customers requested special services, salespeople notified them of the cost of those services. For "A" customers who rarely took advantage of the special emergency efforts (only once every couple of years), the invoice showed the emergency service charge, but right below it showed a "best customer discount" of an equal amount that waived the charge for the first occurrence of the year. The end result gave the service to good customers at no charge—establishing a value for the service while letting the customers know they were important.

For all other customers and prospects, they told them in advance what their policy was so that when a "B," "C," or even "D" customer (or prospect) called in an emergency, there was no surprise when they got the invoice. For "emergency only" customers, the extra charges made it worthwhile to service their special needs. Those customers were still buying most of their supplies from someone else (or they would be an "A" customer), but at least the company made a profit on their occasional business.

This concept had the unexpected result of reducing the number of emergencies. It turned out that many of the calls were not really emergencies after all, but since there was no cost associated with the special handling, certain customers had just been taking advantage of the company.

Second, now that there was a cost associated with the services, it was easier to evaluate the profitability of each customer. If customers used too many special services without charge, it could lower their standing in the internal ratings. This had the effect of reducing the number of specials they received. By arming the salespeople with this knowledge, the customers began to understand the value and better manage their own people to stay in the company's "A" category.

When everyone knows your policy, those who need special services will gladly pay the fee. You will then be rewarded for providing a service your competitor is unable to offer. Additionally, every time a customer uses the service, sales should call on that person. In every case, sales should explain how the company takes care of its "A" customers by letting them know about other services and support the company can provide. In the long run, the company may even gain new "A" customers once they understand the value of an "A" relationship.

Answer: We rebuild pumps for field equipment. Over time, we have learned that after three rebuilds, the fourth one has a much shorter life expectancy and probably should not be done. We do not have a good system for tracking the number of times a pump has been rebuilt and often waste time and money and create field service problems by rebuilding and selling a pump the fourth time.

What was done? This company wanted us to build an automated system to track the pumps and the number of times they were rebuilt. Each pump had a serial number, so the program should have been easy.

The underlying problem was that serial numbers may get worn or broken off during use and are often impossible to read. Furthermore, the tracking cards in the repair room always seemed to be covered in grease and were usually difficult to read.

Adding to the problem, the repair guys were not good at filing, so the old manual cards were almost always lost, misfiled, and impossible to find. There was no reason to expect they would be any better at entering data in a computer system. Plus, whenever there was a problem in the field, they would say, "We just work heads down. We do not have time to try to find the old record to see how many times a pump was rebuilt."

As consultants, we did not believe that designing a new application was the answer. The problem was thrown out to the group of repair people. After a few seconds of thinking, they came up with an answer that was so easy, management was blown away. "Why couldn't we think of that?" was all they could say.

The crew suggested that the company go out and buy three cans of spray paint—green, orange/yellow, and red. When a pump comes in to be rebuilt the first time, they simply clean the top cover (which they do anyway) and spray it green. When a green-topped pump comes in, after the rebuild is complete, they paint it the "ugly yellow." When it shows up a third time, they paint the pump red.

When a red-top pump comes in, the team scavenges certain parts from it (when they have time) that can be reused and toss the rest out. There is almost no time spent tracking the pumps. Now the biggest issue is making sure that there is always a spare can of each color of paint. That is easy.

The company got rid of the tracking cards and the filing system that never worked. Now it is also easier to know when new pumps need to be ordered. Pump life is not a secret. After a red pump goes into the field, the repair guys can tell you almost to the day when it will come back and need to be replaced.

The field guys like the new system because there are fewer problems with short-lived pumps. It is almost impossible to accidentally put very old pumps back in operation. Everyone came out ahead. And it was so simple.

Answer: The inventory levels in the computer are often wrong and therefore not trusted. Whenever there is an order for a product that shows the inventory level is equal to or very close to the ordered amount, we have to get up and walk into the warehouse to make sure the count is accurate. Popular items are often off by one or two, and that destroys our ability to promise and deliver an order. In some cases, when there is just enough product to fill an order, our inside order-entry people will actually pull product off the shelf to hold for a customer order they are working on so it will be there when they finish with the write-up.

What was done? As you may have guessed, our first step was to do a diagnostic to find out why the counts were inaccurate. One cause of the problem was traced to the sales staff going into the warehouse. As a warehouse manager described it, "They drive us crazy. Salespeople come into the warehouse because they want a sample to take to a customer. They refuse to fill out the paperwork to take the item out of stock. The standard excuse is, 'It takes too long and I don't have time to stand around when I can be out making sales.' Then they complain because the stock levels are wrong."

The first easy fix was to set up a simple system in which each salesperson's car or truck was considered a warehouse. Then, a very easy warehouse transfer was done using bar codes and a special ID for each salesperson. They could take any item, and the barcode was read as they left the warehouse along with their ID. (If a company does not have employee badges, they can post the salespeople with their names and barcodes on a sheet that is easily scanned.)

At the end of every period, the sales team was responsible for justifying why they didn't have the inventory anymore. The warehouse kept more accurate counts (so you could believe the system when it said there were four of an item) and there was actually good tracking of all usage.

We found that an additional problem was inaccurate counting when the product was put away, picked, or moved. In this situation, "cycle counting" can be very effective. The computer can determine which items have the most accuracy problems. Following is a process your company can follow if you are facing a similar issue.

Every time an item is picked (or, if it is a high-volume item, only when the amount on the shelf is getting close to the average order quantity), the system requests pickers to count the number of items left on the shelf after pulling their order. This amount is entered into the handheld device that is used to direct the picking.

If the amount entered does not match the system count, a

supervisor is notified and immediately checks the shelf. In cases where the picker miscounted, the number is corrected and the system is known to be in balance. When the count is verified to be incorrect, the new amount is entered and a flag is raised on the item in question.

Items with problematic counts will be counted more frequently to attempt to discover when and why they go out of balance. In some cases, cameras may need to be installed to watch for stealing. Usually, once the word gets out in the company that the inventory is being watched closely, theft goes down and internal accuracy increases.

When an item is accurate for a specific amount of time, it goes off the watch list. By reporting the corrections and publicizing that the inventory is accurate, many of the problems will just go away.

Answer: Meetings always last forever. No matter what has to be done, we always use all the time allotted.

What was done? Over time, this company became so meeting oriented that all meetings took the maximum amount of time. There was always something else to discuss if the work on the agenda got done early. It was dumb to waste the time of people in the room who were not needed for the extended conversation.

First, as an experiment, the company agreed to change the scheduling. To begin with, all meetings were now set to start at an odd number of minutes before or after the hour.

The starting time was also moved as close as possible to the next half hour. This was important because most people scheduled other activities to start on the half hour. The simple changing of the start time to "eleven minutes after 10:00" meant that anyone needing to attend a 10:30 meeting had to be out the door by twenty-five minutes after the hour.

Now the maximum time for the meeting was fourteen minutes. The old half-hour meeting was dead. With that kind of time pressure, people stayed focused to get their part done so they could get out.

Second, people were allowed to leave meetings anytime they did not think they were contributing or getting value from being there. This was a major cultural change and upset some managers who were hurt when attendees left "their" meetings early.

These new rules had many beneficial effects. To begin with, more meetings were started on time with the complete team present. Maybe it was the odd time—people talked about the "weird times" and seemed to be more interested in arriving in a timely fashion.

Next, by starting at an odd number of minutes after the hour (like 10:11 instead of 10:00), the meetings were still finished by 10:25 so the attendees could make their 10:30 meetings (old habits are hard to change), even though those meetings were now probably set for 10:37. In this case, sixteen minutes were saved. Over the course of a month, the number of man-hours recovered was in the hundreds. This became a great example of how to improve operations without any decrement in value produced.

The staff even felt empowered to turn down meeting requests. It took a while for the managers and supervisors to accept the fact that not everyone wanted to attend their meetings to listen to what they had accomplished (that was one of the descriptions of stupid things we accumulated during this project).

Reducing the number of people in meetings, the length of the meetings, and eliminating some meetings completely had a major positive effect on the operations of the company.

Answer: We always have to waste time listening to people read reports bragging about what they accomplished last week.

What was done? This was another meeting-related "dumb" thing. Management thought it was valuable to make sure everyone on a project team knew what was going on. By meeting once a week and allowing everyone to describe what they were working on, they thought the team would be more cohesive and have a better understanding of where they stood on the overall project. An added benefit was that the team members could help one another wherever there were problems.

The staff thought most people did not pay any attention to one another's reports. If you looked closely, everyone in the room—other than the specific person presenting and maybe the project manager—were busy e-mailing and surfing the web on their handheld devices. They all thought they could accomplish more back at their desks.

The solution was to change the format of the meetings. Understanding the desired result from management, we instituted a requirement that all progress reports (which were already being created) be distributed to all meeting attendees at least four hours in advance of the meeting. It would be their responsibility to review the progress reports prior to the start of the meeting.

At the meeting, the first agenda item was to ask if there were any questions on any of the reports. If the answer was no (as was the case at most meetings), then the meeting went on to the second agenda item.

The second item was to ask if any of the attendees who had run into problems or who saw a problem on the horizon wanted to discuss the issue as a group. This provided a forum to assist individuals with the intelligence of the team on an as-needed basis.

The end result was that a meeting that normally lasted over an hour now lasted less than ten minutes on average. The time was still on the calendar and committed to if needed. However, it was used less than once or twice a quarter.

We also found that most issues with the progress reports were resolved prior to the big meeting through one-on-one meetings or conversations. The extra hours returned to the team became valuable time they were able to use for communicating with one another.

Over the course of a year, over 1,800 man-hours were saved. That is almost one full year for a single employee. That is a lot of wasted time that was recovered because someone was willing to identify a stupid thing.

Answer: We allow the salespeople to enter special purchase orders to suppliers, eliminating all control over what is put in inventory. We miss out on price breaks or free shipping when we could have accumulated the special order with one that was being submitted on the same day.

What was done? The sales department stated that the special order customers were always on short fuses, and that salespeople did not have time to wait for a larger order if they were to satisfy the customers. As long as they were making their gross margin contributions, no one should worry about what they were doing or how they accomplished the goal of satisfying the customers.

The reality was not that simple. Salespeople were never charged back for product a customer did not pick up, or for a contract that fell through. The cost of excess inventory was never measured.

Plus, a few customer interviews proved that many "rush" orders were initiated by the sales force and never requested by the customer. When the customer insisted on a special order, it was usually because he or she had experienced multiple late shipments that the salesperson blamed (rightly or wrongly) on purchasing.

The simple answer was that salespeople could order anything they needed, but any inventory that was not sold at or above minimum margins was charged against the salesperson's commission. In addition, inventory that was not picked up by the customer was returned to the supplier and the salesperson's total commission (not just for that order) was reduced by any restocking charges plus inbound and outbound freight.

It may seem like a harsh rule, but it stopped almost all abuses. At least one salesperson quit/was fired over the new policy. In this case, a special purchase was pushed through at the last minute to impact an end-of-the-year bonus. The new process caught the order and highlighted it for examination. When the company's owner called the customer to ask about the order, he found that the customer had not issued a firm purchase request and probably would not need the product for three to six months at the earliest. The owner's reaction against the salesperson was swift and without appeal.

The message to the rest of the sales force was very clear. The salesperson that was fired was not a top performer, but the firing established the fact that top management was serious, and this changed attitudes overnight.

The fix was simple, it was measurable, and it was easily administered. In other words, it worked.

Answer: Whenever purchasing is able to negotiate a special deal, the sales force always gives it away to the customers. Why can't we make extra money?

What was done? Salespeople believe that most customers buy based on price or the knowledge that we are giving them the lowest price available. Many think that if a special deal is negotiated for a "buy," then the extra margin should be given to the customer so they will keep buying.

Studies have disproved this time and time again. So this company decided that purchasing could set up a special account where the value of special purchasing discounts would be placed. That way the accounting was always correct, but the salespeople would see the normal cost on their screens and not a special discounted cost.

The result of this simple change was a larger than expected increase in profits. The salespeople were no longer able to give away the extra margin, and it stayed in the company. As a reward, purchasing was given an end-of-the-year bonus based on the extra dollars of profit they contributed. This encouraged them to work harder and added many more dollars to the bottom line.

SECTION III
The Three Principles

The Three Principles

The best way to establish a culture of improvement is to follow three simple principles:

* KISS is not stupid.
* It is okay to be wrong.
* If it does not add value, do not do it.

These represent many years of field experience. In every case, the principles have been published as articles and taught at conferences around the country. They are now used in college courses and mentoring.

While these principles may seem to be common sense, they are not always followed. Take the time to share them with your teams. Each will help you do a better job implementing changes based on the questions you ask and the answers you get.

CHAPTER 17

KISS Is Not Stupid

There is an old expression that is often used to direct us when we are looking for answers to complex problems. It is called the KISS principle. Many people believe that KISS stands for Keep It Simple, Stupid. To me, people are our most important asset. We are not stupid by nature, and I, for one, resent the implication.

I will admit that some of us do act stupid from time to time. And every one of us can admit to doing something stupid every once in a while. Feeling stupid is a common occurrence. Sometimes we bring it on ourselves. Other times, it sneaks up on us. All in all, it happens more than we might like. However, most of the time we keep it quiet and certainly do not brag about it.

More important, no one likes to have stupidity pointed out, especially in front of others. Foolishness is a private thing.

Any successful team effort starts with respect and mutual goals. The KISS principle is a great way to work together to solve problems. So let us all agree—KISS stands for Keep It Short and Simple.

Encourage brevity. Don't accept shortcuts that reduce quality; instead, strive for effective action that allows you to progress toward goals as quickly as possible with few wasted steps. This is as important in developing systems and procedures as it is in the systems and procedures themselves.

Eliminate complexity. We are no longer trying to get better grades by padding the number of double-spaced typewritten pages we turn in (with extra-wide margins so that we use up more space). The weight of a proposal in response to an RFP is not a valid measure of quality. Looking busy is less important than getting it done right.

We have all seen instances of overly complex processes in the business world. Many of the answers that were provided to the two questions are perfect examples. How much extra effort do we expend in order to band-aid a situation that no longer exists? How many complex systems are designed when using three cans of spray paint can substitute (see the example on pages 94–95)?

Accuracy that cannot be assured with simple measures often gets out of control with complex systems. Adding work to make sure something is done according to the rules (even if outdated) is always much more expensive than setting up methods so that it is done right the first time. Every extra step and every wasted motion adds cost, potential for more errors, reduces morale, and is an additional chance to alienate a good customer.

This leads us to a simple corollary to the KISS principle—make it easy to be right. While working with a client in the '90s, we were looking for ways to improve the company's procedures. In review, we found a process that was much more complex than seemed reasonable.

It turned out that years before, one of the top executives got upset by a mistake that was made. He wanted to make sure it never happened again. Management wrote procedures to add new validation checks. These were created to make sure that, if the situation ever happened again, the error would be caught and corrected. Never again would the mistake be allowed to get out of the office where it could embarrass the executive in charge.

While reviewing this potential area of improvement, one of

the young employees made one of those comments you never forget. Very simply, he asked, "Why do we always make it hard to be wrong instead of easy to be right?"

What a wonderful statement. I have never forgotten it. (Although, I must admit to forgetting the young man's name—so if you are the one who asked this question, please contact me so I can provide proper credit.)

The bottom line is we are always trying to ensure that nothing can go wrong. Well, it can—and it will. The cost to try to prevent every error from occurring is significantly more that the cost of such an error to the operation.

If you are not convinced, try this simple exercise: Take the potential error and calculate the cost of the worst thing that could happen. Then estimate how many times per year this outcome might occur.

Next, look at the process you have created to minimize the occurrence of the problem. Consider all of the costs associated with this process—time, delay in processing, customer aggravation, lost business, and so on. Now estimate the total number of transactions you apply the process to in a year and multiply the two numbers to get an annual cost.

Subtract the cost of the errors occurring from the total cost of trying to prevent them and decide if you are wasting your time. So often we find companies spending tens of thousands of dollars to save hundreds. More important, when examined closely, the number of times the feared error has been caught in the last year (or five years) is often far fewer than the estimated number of occurrences. Frequently, that number is zero.

There is no need to protect yourself from imagined problems that have little effect on the results you are trying to achieve. Look for simplicity and you will be rewarded.

My final advice is to simplify everything. Even plans. Do not try to do too much at once. The more difficult the assignment, the less likely it is to be accomplished. Break down tasks into bite-sized chunks. I normally suggest that most people try to take on tasks of one week or less in duration. That is a time frame you can get your arms around.

It is similar to the Boy Scout method. (I am sure it is the same for Girl Scouts; it is just that I had two boys). We could not give a young child an Eagle Project at age ten. That would guarantee failure and would not build the experience and character the Scouts focus on. The boys started with Skill Awards—something they could do with a parent, at home, in a limited amount of time. It was relatively easy. It taught them they could succeed. It set them up to do bigger and better projects later.

Then we moved them to Merit Badges. These were a bit more difficult. They took more than one evening and required a review by a troop leader. It pushed the Scout out of his comfort zone and offered more lessons about how easy it is to succeed.

Next were rank advancements. These required planning for combinations of Skill Awards, Merit Badges, and reviews by adults and peers in the troop. Scouts learned more lessons at more difficult levels and saw more successes.

Finally, they were ready for an Eagle Project, which required planning, organizing other boys, getting approvals, executing, and then writing up what was done. The final presentation was to a board of unknown leaders—no friendly faces. This was much tougher, involving more lessons and a major undertaking, but led to a major success.

A young Scout could not have done it. It is no different in business. You cannot succeed at doing an Eagle Project your first time. You need to practice. You need to build skills. You need to build confidence. Then you are ready and able to do a project of any size.

Take the time. Learn to do it right. Then get it done. Keep it simple for yourself and everyone on your team. Breaking down the project into weekly segments not only makes it easier for the people responsible for each task, it also makes the project easier to manage.

So make yourself a promise. Simplify everything that you have to do. Break down the tasks that are required. Ask yourself, "What would happen if I did not have to do this step?" Try the process without it. Test things. You will be surprised how much can be accomplished by shortening and simplifying. KISS works, just keep it positive and give it a chance.

CHAPTER 18

It Is Okay to Be Wrong

You need a safe environment if the two questions are going to work. This problem comes from being taught from a very young age that it is bad to be wrong. If people are afraid they will be punished for coming up with a bad idea or one that does not work, they will keep quiet. All of their intelligence and ideas will remain hidden. In over forty years of working, I have learned that the only people who do not make mistakes are those who do not try anything.

Historically, many of the greatest accomplishments have come from making mistakes—and then correcting them when necessary. There are famous stories about Post-it notes (a glue that did not stick), or the "C" grade given to Fred Smith when he described the business outline for Federal Express in a paper at Yale University. Business lore is filled with stories of initial failure followed by tremendous success. All of us share at least a few similar stories of things that did not go well the first time but that led to bigger and better things.

Consider your first time on a two-wheeled bicycle. Unless you were very unusual, you fell. You fell repeatedly. Each fall taught you something. The first few falls were necessary to learn the simple process of keeping your balance. Then your falls helped you learn how to take turns faster and how to handle special situations, like loose stones.

Without a fall, you would have never learned to ride. It is the same in business. You need to try. You need to make mistakes—and then learn from them.

Most of us learned to fear being wrong in grade school. Think back to an early classroom experience. Can you remember an instance where the teacher asked the class a question?

Some student took a chance and raised his or her hand. Then the person gave a wrong answer. Did the teacher congratulate the student for trying?

Probably not. The teacher put his hands on his hips and asked (in a disgusted voice), "Is anyone in the room smart enough to know the right answer?"

After that, who would take a chance? And this did not happen only once. After a while, you would only answer a question if you were absolutely sure of its answer.

Unfortunately, this led us to think we would be better off taking no chances, taking no risks, and being right or being quiet.

In his book *The End of Education,* Neil Postman puts the point this way: "All children enter school as question marks and leave as periods." We actually are beating the creativity out of them.

The only way to correct the situation is to create a new and safe environment. We need to convince our people that it is okay to try. We need to let everyone know that we understand that there is no right or wrong answer when our goal is to brainstorm new answers to old questions.

We will not use everything that is suggested. Some ideas may even elicit laughter, but that is a good sign. It means people are comfortable trying new thoughts. They are not afraid to be wrong. They are willing to stick their necks out and see what comes from a new way of looking at a problem.

This will not be easy. It has to come from the top and filter down through every level of management. There can be no exceptions. It will take time, but it can be accomplished.

Do not blame lack of participation on culture. Culture is not an excuse for doing things poorly. Culture is the glue that holds a team together. Do not confuse closed-minded adherence to "the way we have always done it" with corporate culture. The first is a big negative; the second should be a big positive.

The staff in most companies know how the systems operate. They are aware of the bottlenecks. They know where the confusion occurs. But they are afraid to say anything. What if they are wrong? What if someone else tried to fix something and failed? Why should they take a risk? Usually there are no rewards. There are only (perceived) downsides.

Top managers and the owners of organizations must convince the staff that it is not only safe, but it is part of their duty to find and improve any process that is inefficient or ineffective. Everyone should be encouraged to help improve operations.

Every executive is frequently offered the opportunity to receive tens of thousands of dollars of free consulting. The problem is their egos often get in the way of taking advantage of it. If you are willing to have an open mind and admit that you have been wrong, here is an easy way to gain great insights.

Every time you hire new employees, ask them to visit with you every afternoon during the first two weeks of their employment. Simply ask them the two questions. Encourage them to compare what they see your operation doing with how they did things at their previous jobs.

There are not many people who get invited into the boss's office to tell him or her what dumb things management is doing, so make sure you make them feel safe. This will encourage good feedback. Take every suggestion, idea, or thought and react positively. Follow up. Let them know how much you appreciate the input. Then do something with it.

It is just as important to let them know what you have done. Tell them how you are going to change or that you have done some research, and explain to them the reason for the decision you are making. Every time, thank them and encourage them to come back again and again.

After two weeks, they will be part of the problem. They will have learned how you do things. They will no longer be able to see as clearly as they did when they first arrived. Still, keep the door open for them to visit with you any time they have a thought or question. It is the best input you can get—and you are already paying for it.

So, how do you create a safe environment?

A number of companies have set up an innovation department. The person in charge is responsible for encouraging and developing ideas within the organization. They become the safe set of ears. They run interference. It is their responsibility to make sure that any negatives accrue only to themselves. At the same time, all positives are reflected back to the person who originated the idea.

Over time, it becomes easier. The staff become comfortable. They relax and are more willing to try bringing up new ideas. The number of ideas and their quality will keep improving. Just make sure it is safe and keep the feedback positive.

The head of innovation can also be the facilitator for the ideation meetings where the two questions are asked. They become the face of the corporation and trusted partners.

If this leader is uncomfortable or placed in situations where there is a great deal of negative history to overcome, then an outsider can help people to open up. To build trust, establishing the appropriate ground rules is very important. They may include (and this is a shame) that the boss cannot attend the meeting. As the process proves to be trustworthy (no one gets fired or otherwise penalized for coming up with ideas or suggestions that change something the boss has always done or that he or she designed), the boss may be allowed to attend the next meeting.

In addition to generating great ideas, these meetings will allow management at all levels to learn more about how their staff operates. With observation, they will gain new insights into how things work. The natural leaders will be obvious. Future promotions can be one of the rewards for active participation.

In the meetings, the facilitator's job is to encourage people to share their ideas. He or she has to help everyone understand that ideas are not owned; rather, they are contributed and everyone helps make them better. It is amazing what power that has. Together, your staff will find ways to improve the operation that no individual will ever be able to find alone.

CHAPTER 19

If It Does Not Add Value, Do Not Do It

The last principle builds upon the first two. It may seem to be another one of those overly simplistic rules, but it works and saves much time and effort.

Every operation should have one question asked of it: "Does this operation (step, procedure, expense, effort, etc.) add value to our ultimate customer?" If the answer is no, then do not do it!

There are many situations where you have to carefully weigh nuances, but most of the time, the answer will be unambiguous. Accounts receivable adds value because without it, the company will not be able to generate the cash flow necessary to stay in business.

One company had a process where a copy of all expense reports went to a top manager. When questioned, it turned out this procedure had been initiated years before to make sure no one was cheating the company (actually, one person in particular). No expenses had ever been refused, no expenses had ever been questioned, and no expenses had ever been audited.

Since there was no action being taken, there was no value being added. There was no reason to keep creating, printing, distributing, and then shredding the reports. They did nothing for the end customer.

Over the years, there have been a few "gray" situations. Resolving these types of issues are what top management gets paid for. Consider the example of a "services" department within a company. They were being overwhelmed with work. In order to establish some control, a "chargeback" system was put in place. Now, every department had to spend real budget dollars to get services. This new system quickly reduced the service department's backlog of work.

The amount of work was reduced to the point that the service department was going to be downsized. This fear caused the department to launch a sales effort to the rest of the company to sell more services.

Without the new sales effort, the company did not request as much help as they had once "needed." The service department thought they were helping the company find new opportunities to use automation. It required a tough look at the new requests to see which ones added value to the customers and which ones just added value to the service department. The answers were not always clear.

In every situation, consider the facts carefully. If the added value is not there, do not be afraid to eliminate time, cost, and other resources. If the value is marginal, work to measure what is generated versus the cost. Then make a decision based on the overall value generated.

Stop doing things that do not enhance the customer experience. You will see more dollars going to the bottom line.

EXAMPLES OF THINGS THAT DON'T ADD VALUE

Answer: Every few minutes there is an interruption with an instant message or an e-mail. This happens in meetings (as people monitor their smartphones) and at desks as the arrival of new mail causes an attention-grabbing "bing."

What was done? For most people not in customer service, responding to e-mails and messages as soon as they are received is not required. Some people think they are so important that a momentary delay will cause unknown problems elsewhere in the organization. Actually, that is just a sign of poor management.

In meetings, this company established a new protocol. At all meetings, everyone was to turn off their phones or agree to ignore the (supposedly) silent vibration. The penalty was usually a $1 donation to the "charity of the month" pot.

At the desk, it was suggested that everyone ignore or turn off the notification sound. The company set a standard of checking e-mail no more than once every hour. As people learned that instantaneous responses were not required, the spacing increased to checking only twice per day.

For 99 percent of normal correspondence, the company also set the expectation that all inquiries should be responded to in one business day. The receptionist became the emergency or high-urgency contact. She had permission to contact any person in the company to help a customer. In the rare case that an individual was absolutely required to respond to a situation, the receptionist would find that person.

Answer: When product is received, we wait for the shipping charges before entering the cost so it reflects the total "landed cost" of each item in our inventory.

What was done? For almost all receipts, the approximate shipping cost is easily calculated. There are charts, tables, and computer programs that can give you a very accurate answer based on knowing the weight, size, and the from/to addresses. The answers will normally be within pennies of the actual amount invoiced.

That estimated cost was assigned to the incoming shipment so the new, fully loaded cost could be used in calculating the value of the inventory on the shelf. The total estimated freight was kept in a special "bucket" in the general ledger, and at the end of the year it was compared to the actual inbound freight costs.

The company is considering marking up the estimated freight by 3 percent or 4 percent. This would provide a margin of safety in case there are any significant calculation errors. In the meantime, by increasing the inventory cost, the sales force is getting slightly higher prices to maintain the commission margins. A nice little bonus for getting rid of a dumb thing.

Answer: Customers come to the counter and purchase $10 or $15 worth of goods. Then they tell us to bill it to their account. The counterman was not sure what it really cost the company for him to set up the billing, but he thought it had to be more than the small sale was worth.

What was done? We initiated a short investigation to figure out what it cost to invoice a customer. We took into account all of the paperwork and time to set up an accounts receivable; process the sale (including the cost of the receipt, getting it signed, and filing it in case there was a dispute); the cost of money outstanding for forty-five days; a charge to cover bad debt; the cost of a single follow-up call; and the time to figure out how to apply an unmarked check when it was received without copies of the various sales invoices.

Each company will be different. In this case, the total cost was just over $50. Studies show costs as high as $85 and as low as $30 at other organizations.

Then we looked at average gross margin (the value of the sale less the cost of goods sold) and found it to be about 40 percent in this situation. (Again, this number will vary widely based on the industry, geographic location, and service levels.) A simple calculation showed that we needed to sell at least $125 just to cover the cost of invoicing—without any income left for overhead, salaries, or to purchase the product, let alone profits. That means the company lost money on all of those small sales.

One idea was to require all smaller sales to be paid by credit card. Accounting was initially concerned that the higher charges for using credit cards would have a negative impact on their profitability.

The sales staff was concerned that if we did not continue to provide an invoicing capability, we would lose a great number of high-value customers. After all, competitors offered invoicing and terms, so how could we not?

Everyone realized that sales had a strong point. As a result, the customer base was divided into two groups. The first were "A" customers who purchased over $5,000 per month. These customers were allowed to continue to charge purchases at the counter. All others were asked to use a credit card, cash, or a check for any amount under $200. If someone complained, the supervisor on duty could do an override.

Most people did not complain at all. They were very happy to get their frequent flyer mileage using a credit card, and many companies even had company cards that rewarded the owners.

The other "surprise" to accounting was that the credit card charges for a small sale lost significantly less money than the cost of doing our own invoicing. Since the charges are a function of the size of the sale, the company is keeping an eye on the process and will institute an upper limit if that becomes an issue in the future.

As a result of this change, the company has found it gets paid a great deal faster and bad debt is down. (Most of the individual trouble was from small accounts.) Counter sales move faster and there is much less paperwork.

Answer: We spend more to deliver product to a customer than it would cost if we used UPS or a delivery service.

What was done? When the cost of maintaining delivery trucks was calculated, the ownership group almost had a fit. No one had ever really dug into the real cost of delivery. It was just one of those things you had to do to be in business. As long as there was a profit at the end of the year, it was assumed all costs were being properly covered.

With the cost of delivery so high, the company decided to get out of the delivery business. They contracted with a local delivery service and eliminated a couple of trucks and drivers (plus the cost of repairs, insurance, and storage).

The customers were told they could come by the warehouse to pick up the needed part at no extra cost, or we could send it to them by courier or local delivery truck at *their* expense. The delivery service charged the customer cash or by credit card, so there was no extra paperwork by the company.

Of course, exceptions were made for "A" customers who had special needs. Over time, however, many of them were willing to pay for the delivery as a convenience.

Answer: We spend more time and effort serving some of our "internal" customers than makes sense for the ultimate customer.

What was done? Some people will want to argue that they have internal customers that are just as important. I disagree. If your internal customers are wasting time and effort, it just impairs your ability to generate desired results.

If your energy is going to support an activity that does not ultimately benefit your customer, then why do it? You need to focus all your energies on the ultimate customer. In a down economy, there is a great value to focused effort. Know what makes your customers happy so that they keep buying from you. Do that better than anyone else in the industry and your future will be secure.

Some people ask me why we are willing to help accounts receivable do a better job. The answer is that it ultimately serves the customer. You need to collect money to be able to continue to provide products and services. Making accounts receivable more efficient will allow you to spend less money collecting revenue and that, in turn, may allow you to offer lower prices. If you decide to keep the savings as part of your profit, it will provide a return so that you can stay in business.

Keep your focus on the customer and you will do well.

Conclusion

As this book comes to an end, I hope you have been energized to look for ways to improve your business. I hope you have found positive alternative methods to encourage your employees to look for new and better ways to do everything.

We are in an unusual economic time as I write this. Managers can apply the ideas and concepts in this book to discover another way to do old things. Each change is an opportunity to do things better, faster, more efficiently, and more effectively.

My experience tells me the lessons in this book can be applied to any business or not-for-profit organization to allow them to do more with less. Even after the current crisis passes, there will still be opportunities to improve operations. Any time we can apply extra resources to important activities, we are better off.

In most downturns, the first thought is to cut. Random cutting may do more harm than good. Focus yourself by understanding what it is that really needs to be done and how to do it. Get rid of the dumb and difficult chores. Do everything possible to get more things done with less "doing."

Even when things are going well, don't lose your opportunity to use the methods in this book. Make things better. Use the benefit of available resources to prepare for the next downturn. (Yes, they will continue to happen.) Your efforts will be rewarded with additional profits. Keep the money, invest in new things, or give some to charity. Support the community that supports you.

Remember that by leaving the "do-do" world behind, you can move to a "done-done" environment where action generates results. Stop running in circles and get things done. You will be amazed at the difference it makes.

Extras

How to Hold a Meeting

There are a few procedural guidelines to holding a meeting that will help you be successful.

Meetings and retreats are used for many different purposes. Sometimes they are used to inform a group about decisions that have been made. Other times they are used to develop the strategic or tactical questions that must be answered prior to announcing results internally or to the public. For this process, most meetings can be very informal. In some cases, brainstorming-type meetings are best held where the environment is conducive to thinking and away from the day-to-day pressures of work.

The meeting environment may be ignored for ad hoc meetings or situations where a very short meeting time is required. Just about any reasonable meeting space can be made to work. If the discussion will be longer, more spirited (a nice way to say argumentative), and have serious long-term consequences for the organization, then control of the environment is important.

Once you have identified a number of answers to the two questions, your organization has an opportunity to create new methods and procedures that can fundamentally change the way it operates. Even better, it can change the competitive equation in the marketplace. Finding those fantastic answers requires a specific environment for success.

The environment includes all of the factors surrounding the physical setting of the meeting. It can also include general rules of the meeting. These help set the tone and can greatly influence the results.

As social beings, getting together is important whenever we have to work out differences, resolve issues, or attempt to look into the future. Our meetings can succeed or fail for numerous reasons. The objective here is to eliminate the environment as a cause of failure.

As with any prescriptive advice, there is always a caveat. When dealing with human beings, there are few absolute answers. If you are uncomfortable with any aspect of the following recommendation, change it. This is not an all-or-nothing set of suggestions. Use what makes sense to you with your group, your situation, and your budget.

Setting up an environment for success may not be difficult, but it is vitally important. While none of the following suggestions are very involved, it takes time and money to do them all. Some meetings may be held at the last minute and some groups will have little or no leeway on where to meet or how much money can be spent. Not every aspect of the perfect meeting can be followed in every situation. Do what you can. These ideas do work and have been proven over many years.

Circumstances and budgets have forced all of us to hold meetings in less than ideal environments. A less than perfect meeting space may add a level of complexity and make the facilitator's job more difficult. It does not make it impossible. Just remember, small changes to the environment can have a big impact on the outcome of any meeting. Do what you can and take advantage of these easy ideas.

LOCATION

The meeting location sets the stage for everything that comes after. Therefore, the first order of business is to determine where to hold the meeting. The choices are really very few. There are meeting rooms at the office, in restaurants, or at hotels and resorts. Each type of location offers advantages, disadvantages, and various levels of cost. If your organization has sufficient space and the staff can separate themselves from normal activities, onsite meetings may be your best and usually least expensive option.

Here, we are interested in business meetings for questioning how we do things. We will be looking for new answers to old questions. Do not invite guests or extraneous staff. All attendees should be stakeholders in the questions and the results.

An office, for all of its positives, may not be the best choice if employees will be prone to interruptions from phone calls, people who just happen to drop by, and sudden emergencies ("As long as you are here, can you take just a second to . . ."). Using onsite office space requires discipline to treat the attendees as if they are out of the office and cannot be found or interrupted.

Restaurants are OK for shorter meetings and working meals. The chairs tend to be harder, the spaces less soundproof (i.e., you can be disturbed by groups next door), and the lighting may be dimmer. One offsetting consideration is the added perk of lunch or dinner, which is usually a big plus for the attendees. It makes them feel special and valued.

Restaurants are not known for having lots of workspace. If

you expect that people may need to take notes, shuffle stacks of paper, or spread out, there may be better environments, and you could always cater a meal if providing food is a priority. This does not mean that meeting for a meal in a restaurant or hotel setting will not work, just plan to use the meeting for a discussion topic where one person per table can be appointed to take notes. Then review what was discovered when you reconvene in the more traditional meeting room.

Check every space for quietness. Whenever possible, insist on an empty room between you and the nearest activity or other meeting. Do not accept rooms near a live band or DJ. Be especially careful of nearby large group meetings. They often tend to be loud and will interfere with what you are doing.

Hotels and resorts normally provide the best meeting options when long, multiple-day meetings are held, but they are usually the most expensive. They can be flexible in terms of furniture, room arrangement, and special setups. There is a degree of ease when one organization can arrange for your meals, beverages, and overnight services for multiple-day retreats. Do not reject this option out of hand. You may be surprised at the special deals you can get, especially at city-center business locations over a weekend.

Be wary of fancy resorts, as these can sometimes confuse the focus of the meeting. If everyone is chomping at the bit to get out to a famous golf course, they will not be concentrating on the business of the organization. Once again, know your group and their desires.

There are exceptions to every rule, but for most meetings, the location should be easy and convenient to get to. If your attendees are flying in from regional operations, facilities near airports with free transportation are always winners. Pick airports that most of the participants can get to nonstop.

Always make an in-person visit to any site. Pictures and brochures do not tell the real story. See the room you will meet in, see where you will eat, and if overnight accommodations are to be used, see the rooms. Check for Americans with Disabilities Act compliance, especially if you know attendees will be using wheelchairs or needing other assistance. It is your responsibility to make sure everything is top-notch and works for your group.

THE ROOM

The meeting space itself needs to be large enough for comfort and have room in which to "move." Oddly shaped rooms may look good in pictures but seldom work as well as a traditional square or rectangle. When there are less than eight people, almost any board-type room with an oval or rectangular table will work. Groups of over twenty require many special arrangements (and are beyond the scope of this chapter). The following guidelines will work best for groups between eight and twenty.

Our experience suggests that thirty linear inches is a reasonable amount of space per person at a table. Therefore, eight people (four on each side) need a table at least ten feet long. This may seem large, but if you are going to be sitting there for eight to ten hours, the space is necessary. Twenty-four inches is the minimum to be able to do anything, but it is not as comfortable, provides little "personal space," and certainly will not be conducive to a robust discussion.

Space is necessary between the sides of the table and the walls so people can move around. A good minimum is three feet from the table to the nearest wall. That way, someone can squeeze behind a participant sitting at the table.

If there is enough space, a coffee break service in the room is a wonderful perk. The longer the meeting, the more necessary it is. There should be space to stand at the coffee service without interfering with any participant. Some meeting rooms have a service bar built in. These take up little meeting space and are very effective.

At the front of the room, space for a facilitator to work and write on easels requires five to six feet in front of any meeting table. The facilitator will often have a chair for meals, but it is usually pushed under the table or kept out of the way during most of the meeting.

When determining the setup for the room, windows and doors can be a problem. The best setup is for the door to be at the back of the room. That way, attendees can enter and leave without disturbing the meeting (or at least minimize the disturbance).

Windows should also be at the back of the room or have drapes/shades that can be pulled. There is nothing worse than a meeting where the participants are looking out on a sunny day with a beach or mountains in view. Their attention will constantly be a million miles away. Uncovered windows at the front of the room are to be avoided at all costs. No one can look at a "backlit" facilitator for very long.

The temperature of the room will never be right for everyone. A simple rule of thumb is that it's always better to err a bit cooler than hotter. Most of us can add a sweater if we get a little chilled (I am not talking about keeping the thermostat at 40 degrees), but there is a limit to what we can remove if it gets too warm. Plus warmer temperatures encourage sleep.

If you have a thermostat in the room, put one person in control. If everyone is jumping up to swing the setting from one extreme to the other, you end up with anarchy and a very uncomfortable, distracted meeting.

Lighting is the other variable that makes a big difference. Bright light keeps everyone more awake and alert. If your meeting requires a projector, try to turn off (or unscrew) the light bulbs that are right above the screen. That way, you can eliminate the glare on the screen but keep the working space well lit. Remember, dimmed lights (like too warm a temperature) encourage sleep.

Should there be a clock in the room? Since just about everyone will have a watch, you are not going to keep the time a secret. However, the preference is to have the clock, if there is one, in the back of the room. It becomes the official clock and can be used for timing specific discussions or to determine returns from breaks.

(One way I get everyone back on time after a break or meal is to set the expectation based on the official clock—my watch if there is no clock in the room; I always pick an odd time like seventeen minutes after the hour—it is easier to remember. Then, if anyone is late, he or she has to tell a joke to the rest of the group; not a big penalty, but it is one that seems to work.)

SETUP

The actual setup of the meeting space will affect the levels and types of interaction. In a small group, keep everyone close. For three to six people, small round tables work well. Six to nine people can meet at a boardroom table. For groups over ten (and even for some groups as small as eight), the "U" or horseshoe shape is the most effective. There is more room to spread out and the seating is more flexible, which makes facilitating the meeting easier. A meeting of twenty people can be easily managed with this setup.

No matter which configuration you use, be very careful about where people sit. Do not allow the participants to create "us and them" seating. This will immediately instigate confrontation and is to be avoided at all costs. Assign seats so that the "departments" will be mixed up. It forces conversation and reduces rancor. (See the next discussion, "Seating Assignments," for a more detailed review of the issues and suggestions.)

Whenever possible, use tables that are at least thirty inches deep. The extra room is worthwhile and provides sufficient space for food, drink, notes, and laptop computers. Arrange for a power strip in the center if laptops will be used during the meeting. Tripping over cords stretched out behind the seating is dangerous for people and computers.

Then, provide enough room for the facilitator to move comfortably in the middle of the "U." Good facilitators know how to use this space to defuse conflict and to encourage discussion. At least four feet is required between the legs of the "U."

The chairs should be as comfortable as possible. Chairs on wheels that can tilt, have a height adjustment, and can swivel are best. Inexpensive stacking chairs do not work as well. They are uncomfortable and increase fatigue just when you need everyone's fullest attention. If folding chairs are the only option, include more frequent breaks. If at all possible, give participants a reason or permission to move around the space and stretch.

Some facilities can provide a sofa or two in the room. Smaller, informal groups appreciate the ability to be more comfortable. Giving people the ability to change their location can improve the conversation.

SEATING ASSIGNMENTS

Probably the most overlooked environmental aspect of the meeting is assigned seating. Most meetings allow random seating based on "first come, first served." This approach leaves your meeting's success to chance. People will select their seats by cliques and egocentric arrangements that can reduce communication and encourage factionalism.

In advance of the meeting, establish a seating chart. Do not leave it to chance. There are a few simple rules that will improve the meeting. First, people who work together or are "best friends" should *not* be allowed to sit next to one another. This rule will minimize side conversations. Next, make sure your people do not sit by rank and reporting relationship. If there are "sides," make sure they are interspersed. Separate power players and spread them around.

Then, recognize that specific seats have differing amounts of power associated with them (see figure 1). Put your most powerful attendees in the weakest seats. It allows the facilitator to control their contribution as opposed to fighting against them if they attempt to overwhelm the meeting. By the same token, placing your shy or less vocal participants in the strong seats helps them be heard. It is easier to draw out their ideas and comments.

Figure 1: Seating Diagram

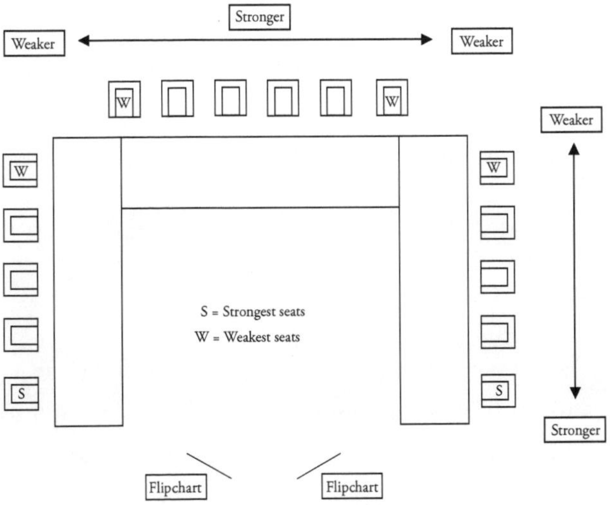

If there will be working meals in a separate room, arrange seating for that location as well. The same types of rules apply. Any time you want to have open discussion or idea generation, mixing people up encourages new input and viewpoints. If you need to make decisions or want to take specific actions, however, then grouping people by department, responsibility, or rank may be appropriate.

Set the room with name tents so everyone will know where they are to sit. Tents can be made out of any paper, but a heavier card stock is better. You can hand print first names in large letters or have a computer print the names in 70-point (or larger) type. This is the easiest way to get people to go where you want them. Always bring a couple of blanks and a large marker pen for the inevitable correction, new person, or unexpected guest.

Name tents have the added advantage of helping the facilitator remember names. If your group meets infrequently or has many new faces, name tents help everyone get to know one another. Including the names on the backs of the tents will help each person's neighbor get the names right as well.

Use special markings (Group A, B, or C; Meal Table 1, 2, or 3) on the inside of the tent to indicate where each person is to sit for breaks, meals, or other functions. Then have identifiers that match the codes on the tables to be used. This is an easy way to control the groups for break sessions and to encourage "mingling" during meals.

TIMING

Time is so very important in our busy lives. Time away from work can be intimidating to some, loathed by workaholics, and a vacation to others. A small amount of consideration will go a long way toward increasing the effectiveness of any meeting.

To begin with, Monday mornings are tough for many people. They want to be able to get their teams started for the week and catch up on weekend activities before being out of the office for a full day or more. If they are flying in, missing Sunday dinner with the family is another imposition that may not be appreciated. Friday afternoons are another time to avoid. The mind leaves for the weekend long before the body can join. Use Fridays only in conjunction with a full-weekend meeting.

When possible, start morning meetings before the business day begins. Any meeting that starts after the beginning of the day will start late. It is almost an unwritten rule of life. If you give busy people the opportunity to go to their desks before going to the meeting, something will delay them—guaranteed. Start with a light breakfast for the early risers to give them a reason to miss traffic if driving to the meeting location. Do not start the meeting later than 8:00 a.m. if you want to begin on time.

Lunch is another good starting time. It is a natural break in the day, and people will usually find they can leave to get to your meeting on time. Call the lunch for 11:30 and beat the lunch-time traffic. The actual meeting may not start until 1:00, but by then everyone (even the "always late" people) will be there and ready to go.

The best afternoon time is 3:00 or 3:30, especially if the meeting will go into the evening. This gives people time to get most of their work done for the day and still avoid rush hour traffic to get to the meeting location. If people are flying in, it saves an extra overnight away from home and allows all but the West Coast to East Coast flyers time to get there easily on the same day. Just as with lunch, start with a coffee/cookie break so there is a buffer to reward the "on-timers" while waiting for the later arrivals.

Even though you have set the time, what do you do when some attendees are late? One option is to set up the expectation of a penalty in advance. A donation to a charitable organization is a good idea. The big question is when do you really start? What if one of the executives is late? What do you do? Waste everyone's time while you wait for the leader to show up or try to start the meeting missing one of the most important participants? The right answer is to start the meeting. Even executives can get the message and if there's a consequence, they will be on time the next time.

One sneaky way I try to keep from being in that position is to call a special meeting of the executive leadership just prior to the main meeting. My goal is to have all of the critical ears at the meeting location an hour ahead of the start time for critical meetings. If it is an 8:00 a.m. meeting, we will have an executive breakfast at 7:00. Some people are just always late—work around them as much as possible.

Finally, watch out for holidays, especially the religious kind. Many meetings have become disasters because the date was picked without regard for the tremendous diversity in our workforce today. The very people who will be offended may not recognize a conflicting date in advance and only realize they cannot attend at the last minute. Then they wonder if you did not care about their participation or are prejudiced against their group. Check the calendar carefully and specifically ask about upcoming celebrations.

Breaks are another important issue. If there are smokers in the group, then breaks may have to be more often and longer or you will lose their input. Normally, a good facilitator will recognize the need for a break and call one as necessary. We normally agree in advance that everyone will break at the same time. Our rule is anyone can request a break and then we all go at once. It minimizes the distractions and keeps everyone present in all the discussions.

A good rule of thumb is that a break should be taken at least every ninety minutes. Five to ten minutes is a reasonable length of time for most breaks. If it is longer, you will lose attendees to phone calls and emergencies that they had time to discover. When your participants are sitting on hard chairs or the environment is less than ideal, more frequent stretch breaks are most appreciated by all of the attendees.

Meal breaks are usually thirty to forty-five minutes. A working lunch or dinner may last longer, but always allow an extra fifteen minutes after every meal for nature breaks and for people to move around without the group. Do not serve alcohol at any meal where you will want people to return to the meeting after eating.

When possible, a coffee break service should be in the room at all times. Today, it is important to include regular and decaf coffee; regular, diet, and decaf soda; regular and decaf tea; and bottled water. In the morning, provide some type of pastry choice (donuts, pound cake, or bread/bagels). An hour or so after lunch, bring out an assortment of cookies (chocolate chip if I am your facilitator) or sweets to raise blood sugar levels. Munchies for meetings after dinner depend on the individuals in the group. Fresh fruit is appreciated all day long.

MEALS

A whole book could be written on meals at meetings. Following are a few simple suggestions to consider. Begin by surveying (or knowing well) all of the attendees to discover their eating preferences. Make sure you know about any special dietary needs (e.g., kosher, diabetic, vegetarian, low-sodium, etc.).

Next, keep all meals light. Serve a full steak dinner for lunch and watch your attendees sleep most of the afternoon. Sandwich and salad buffets are nice and give everyone a choice of what to eat. Breakfast buffets work as well. Oatmeal is very appreciated by attendees who watch their cholesterol. Juices should include at least one alternative to orange.

If you want to work through meals, consider using that time for discussions. Have each table report back to the group after the meal is done. It is a great break from the meeting routine and encourages people to meet others if you mix up the seating.

Beat the hunger pains if at all possible. That means you should serve breakfast as early as people can be expected to arrive. Lunchtime should start between 11:30 a.m. and noon. Dinner is appropriate any time after 5:00 p.m. If space and the agenda allow, have the meals in a different room. The change of environment is invigorating for the mind and helps people perform at their best.

PROPS

Most meetings of the type we are discussing require a few pieces of special equipment to organize the effort and help them run smoothly. Flip charts are the most used item. For most situations, two easels are best. One is used for keeping notes and the second is an "idea parking lot" to capture great thoughts for later discussion. The second easel also allows you to be prepared if the first one runs out of paper without interrupting the meeting to reload.

There are many types of paper you can use. Standard-sized flip charts are not standard but can easily be found in twenty-seven-by-thirty-four-inch pads. Some people prefer to have lines or squares preprinted to make it easier to write in straight lines. Check with the meeting leader or facilitator for his or her preference. Then make sure you start with a (relatively) full pad. Keep the "one or two sheets left" pads for use at the office.

Since most flip chart writing ends up on a wall somewhere, either Post-it note–type sheets, "static cling" sheets, or masking tape will be necessary. Check with the facility to see if they have rules against using tape on their walls, wallpaper, or painted surfaces.

Also check that the paper is of a sufficient weight (thickness). That way, you can write on a sheet already hanging on the wall without leaving a reminder of your visit behind the sheet. Cleaning wallpaper can be very expensive.

There should be a set of at least three colored and one black marker. The longer the retreat, the more important it is to have spares. If the facility has a white board, be careful not to use permanent markers on their board.

As a quick hint to make life after the meeting easier, number each sheet as you start it in the upper right corner. This will help you get all of the charts in chronological order no matter how many you have used or where they end up on the wall.

Some meetings use electronic white boards so that copies of all notes can be produced (without transcription) for each attendee—while at the meeting. These are nice, but at the end of the meeting, you may not have all the notes that were added by individuals after a sheet was handed out.

Another prop that has become common in many environments is the "talk ball." All too often, people like to interrupt or carry on multiple conversations. A simple ball, toy animal, or other fun prop can be used to designate who has the floor. Until that item is passed, no one else can speak. This makes it easier for people to collect their thoughts in order to finish a statement without worrying that someone else will jump in if there is one-half second of silence.

Other toys can be used effectively if there are high levels of tension. People can be given "smiles" on a stick to wave when being facetious (like a ☺ at the end of an e-mail).

FINAL TIPS

Here are a few final ideas to help make the meeting as successful as possible. Each will improve the environment for thinking and contributing:

- **Have all beepers, cell phones, and wireless e-mail devices turned off!** If people absolutely need to be reachable, set the device to vibrate. Ask them to alert their staff and family that they are at an important meeting and are only to be interrupted for a real emergency. Remember, any interruption is an excuse to leave the meeting. Arrange for the meeting facility to accept calls (if available) and take messages. These can be brought to the room in an emergency. Otherwise, they should be taped outside the door to be picked up at breaks.

- **All egos and titles are checked at the door.** Most idea-generating meetings depend on sharing. If one or two people are going to be allowed to dictate the answers, then why hold the meeting? Everyone should have something to add or you are inviting the wrong people. Inside the room, the playing field must be level if you are to get the most value from your attendees.

- **There is only one conversation at a time.** Very few people can keep up with and participate in multiple discussions at once. And it is impolite to ignore what another person believes to be an intelligent addition to the discussion. Let everyone have his or her say and rely on a professional facilitator to control the time everyone takes.

- **Break together.** The mood is easily broken if people are constantly getting up and leaving the room. This may even encourage conversations outside of the room and destroy the advantage of meeting together. Do not lose anyone's participation. When people need a break, let them request it. Then everyone goes and returns at the same time, which makes it easier to build consensus and a "team" atmosphere.

- **Prior to the meeting, send a formal invitation.** Include the agenda to be followed, a list of the objectives, all meeting details (time, location, instructions for parking, and where to have messages sent), and any "homework" that is to be done in advance.

- **Have pencils, pens, and paper for the attendees.** It is almost inconceivable that an otherwise intelligent employee would come to a meeting unprepared, but it happens all the time. If documents were distributed in advance for review, have extra copies to hand out onsite.

- **Provide a report at the conclusion of the meeting.** Include copies of flip charts or a summary of what was accomplished. Know your audience and take care of people's needs. This includes all the people who did not participate but will be affected by the outcome.

While the best environment in the world will not save a poorly conceived or mismanaged meeting, it can greatly enhance the potential for success.

Opportunity in the Ordinary

We miss opportunities all the time. Everyone is interested in hitting the home run. Wouldn't it be nice to initiate the disruptive change that moves the industry to a new paradigm? We all wish we could find the next *big* thing before anyone else. There are plenty of little things out there that will pay big benefits and outsized returns. We just need to be willing to open our eyes and our minds to new possibilities.

One simple story is about Robert Fishbone, an innovative percussionist. He was intrigued by an instrument called a spring drum.

Remo Belli, the owner of Remo, Inc., and one of the developers of the game-changing artificial drumhead, saw Robert at a percussionist show and was impressed with the unique designs Robert was selling. Remo invited Robert to California to look at a new project he was working on, the spring drum. It was about twelve inches in diameter and had a drumhead across one end with a spring hanging from it. When moved properly, it made a deep thunder sound.

He knew that Robert was already very successful selling to the novelty gift market, which was much larger than the market for musicians. He asked if there was some way spring drums could be sold to a broader market.

Robert experimented and worked to make the tube smaller so it would fit in a child's hand, painted it with lightning bolts, and renamed it the Thunder Tube. He proceeded to sell over one hundred thousand.

It was an ordinary invention—no electronics, nothing fancy. It was designed for a specific use, and the original developer could not see beyond its initial purpose. Luckily, he recognized that fact and took advantage of a chance meeting to bring in a talented outsider at the first opportunity.

Remo was so impressed with how well the Thunder Tube outsold Spring Drums that his company licensed it back from Robert, who now gets a royalty on every one that is sold to any of their customers.

Robert expanded the market from musicians and formal orchestras to include

- The toy marketplace
- Film, radio, theater, and puppet show industries (to use as device to create sound effects)
- Storytellers
- Science teachers
- People who work with autistic children
- People who work with animals (especially horses) to desensitize them to loud noises, including thunder

When an outsider looked at the instrument, he saw a new opportunity. He saw possibilities the owner of the invention could not see. To use an overworked term, this is the power (negative power) of paradigms. They keep people from seeing the possibilities. Once released from established constraints, the ideas pour in.

How many ordinary things do we see every day that could become the foundation of a new business or open up new markets? New products, new services, and new opportunities are all around us. Keeping your eyes wide open is the key to finding the opportunity in the ordinary.

Hints for Employees with Good Ideas

So, you have a great idea—now what do you do with it? If we assume that your corporate culture is not really conducive to new ideas coming "from below," you will need to find a safer way to take an idea up the line.

Start by realizing that lots of people have good ideas. Only a very few are willing to get behind their ideas and take them somewhere. By choosing to share your idea, you are already ahead of the crowd.

Take any idea and think through it in detail, over and over again. Rarely are the best ideas the first thing out of someone's mind. Initial thoughts *are* the genesis of the right thing to do, but they may require a number of iterations before reaching their final form.

The best way to go from an idea to an inspiration is to put together a small group of peers—your coworkers who have an interest in improving things. The best groups are diverse and include people from all areas that will be affected (positively and negatively) by the new idea.

As an alternative, you can do the same thing with a mentor

or friendly supervisor. Let that person help you get the idea off the ground. They may even want to bring in a few other people at higher levels. Do not be intimidated. Your ideas and knowledge are just as valuable as theirs. They may have different insights and these can help the idea become better and more successful.

Make sure everyone knows this is not a sanctioned project and that it must be kept confidential until it is ready for disclosure. That means you have to pick your team carefully. When possible, have at least one long-term employee who understands and can navigate the political landscape. He or she will be an invaluable resource as you move forward.

Use this group as a sounding board. Get together outside of work. Find a time and place where you can work without interruption for at least two or three hours. Pull up a bunch of comfortable chairs. Maybe have a flip chart, or at least lots of blank paper to draw and write on. Introduce the problem and your first thoughts about how to solve it. Then (and this is the secret sauce—and the hardest thing for most humans to do) let go and watch what happens.

Our first inclination is to defend our original position. *Do not!* It will stop all creativity in an instant. As a matter of fact, before the brainstorming begins, ask all participants to check their egos at the door. Explain that there is no individual ownership of the idea, but that together as a group you will come up with something better than any individual could.

Hash out the ideas. Take all input. Revise the questions and the answers. Look at it from the viewpoint of everyone who will be affected. Try to answer questions before they can be asked.

Do not be discouraged if more than one meeting is required to get where you want to go. Know that everyone will have things to add. Just do your best to stay focused on the issue at hand. Put everything else on a flip chart or pad of paper labeled "The Idea Parking Lot."

For every problem (opportunity) there is a primary customer. Figure out who that is. Sometimes it is the government, sometimes a supplier, or the normal end user of your product or service. Whoever it is, make sure you know how they use what the company normally delivers to them. Understanding how they use a product or information will allow you to cut out unnecessary work and focus on what is important to them.

As the idea develops, ask the group to help define the metric of your success. Every time you have to sell something "up the line," you have to be able to explain how the operation will recognize success. It does not work to say, "Trust us, it will work." There have to be specifics.

Sometimes the step of deciding what to measure is the most difficult. Review chapter 5 on metrics. It will give you more ways to think about the possibilities. You will need to be able to explain how the top management team can tell if the new process is working.

Next, it is important to understand the people you will be presenting the idea to. All executives have personality styles. Present to their specific style and you will automatically do better. If they are drivers, they will want to get to the bottom line quickly. Some people will want to know all the background to make sure you did your homework. Others may only want to see the big picture and then move on.

Know your audience and play to them. If multiple types will be in attendance, be prepared to work with all of them. Make sure what they need is in the handouts and offer to spend time reviewing all the details with anyone who would like extra explanations.

Finally, make sure the presentation keeps focused on why

your idea is valuable. What is the benefit to the executive you are asking to sponsor a new project, invest limited resources, and stick his or her neck out to test your idea?

Before the meeting, practice with your team of advisers. Make sure you know the material cold. Have them hit you with all the tough questions. Try to anticipate anything that could go wrong and prepare an answer or work-around.

Make sure you always end the meeting on time and do not forget to *ask* for something. It can be funding, it can be another meeting, or it can just be permission to continue to develop the idea. Whatever it is, do not forget to ask for it. Many projects die because there is no action item to keep the idea alive. Do not let this happen to you.

After the meeting, send all attendees a thank-you note or e-mail to let them know you appreciated their time. In the note, include any approved next steps, a tentative schedule, and information about when you will get back in touch with them.

All that remains is for you to follow through and execute. Put all the pieces together and watch your reputation grow.

About the Author

 Steve Epner, a pioneer in the world of computers, wrote his first program at the Illinois Institute of Technology in 1965. He graduated from Purdue University in 1970 with a degree in computer science and founded his own consulting company, User Group, Inc., in 1976. User Group completed a merger with Brown Smith Wallace, LLC, a business and financial advisory firm, in 2005. For over two decades, Epner has published the Distribution Software Guide (available online at www.software4distributors.com), which is now provided as a membership benefit to members of over fifty trade associations. In 2007, Epner earned a master of science from the Purdue University College of Technology and was appointed the Innovator in Residence at Saint Louis University.

Epner's unique ability to make complex concepts understandable for busy executives—and his understanding that technology alone doesn't solve real business problems—has made him a sought-after adviser and speaker. He has served as a faculty member for the University of Industrial Distribution and for the Manufacturers' Representatives Education and Research Foundation, and he is a faculty member at Saint Louis University in the Graduate School of Business and the Center for Supply Chain Management Studies. Epner also teaches innovation in the undergraduate business school at Webster University, and has published over one thousand articles and made over four hundred professional presentations. This is his ninth book.

Steve Epner is the reality check you need to get your team from do-do to done-done. Steve has worked with people and multinational companies across the continent and is frequently requested to Simplify Everything through:

- Formal presentations (from 45-minute keynotes to full-day workshops)
- Facilitation (including planning for single- or multi-day retreats covering strategy, process improvement, or just basic idea generation)
- Rolling up his sleeves and working with teams on site
- Executive level coaching and support

Stop thinking and start doing by contacting Steve to get it DONE! Steve@SteveEpner.com

Made in the USA
Charleston, SC
06 June 2013